ALIVE AT THE VILLAGE VANGUARD
MY LIFE IN AND OUT OF JAZZ TIME

ALIVE
AT THE
VILLAGE
VANGUARD

MY LIFE IN AND OUT OF JAZZ TIME

BY LORRAINE GORDON

AS TOLD TO BARRY SINGER

End sheet art by Paul Petroff.
Photos on pages 64 and 69 by William P. Gottlieb.
Photos on page 115 and 189 by Gene Cook.
Photo on page 185 by Nancy Miller Elliott.
Photo on page 209 by Y. Yanagi.

Book interior by Mark Lerner.

Published by Hal Leonard Corporation
7777 Bluemound Road
P.O. Box 13819
Milwaukee, WI 53213

Trade Book Division Editorial Offices
19 West 21st Street
Suite 201
New York, New York 10010

Library of Congress Cataloging-in-Publication Data

Gordon, Lorraine.
  Alive at the Village Vanguard : my life in and out of jazz times / by Lorraine Gordon as told to Barry Singer. — 1st ed.
     p. cm.
  Includes index.
  ISBN-10 0-634-07399-0
  ISBN-13 978-0-634-07399-1
  1. Village Vanguard (Nightclub) 2. Gordon, Lorraine. I. Singer, Barry. II. Title.
  PN1968.U5G58 2006
  792.709747'1—dc22
                        2006021350

Printed in the United States of America

First Edition

Hal Leonard books are available at your local bookstore, or you may order through Music Dispatch at 1-800-637-2852 or www.musicdispatch.com.

CONTENTS

ACKNOWLEDGMENTS

With special thanks to Rebecca, Deborah, Joan, Antonio, Helene Greece, Fletcher Roberts, Loretta, Lea, and Sara.

And my cast of characters at the Vanguard:
Jed Eisenman, and Mady Abel, Eric Baltazar, Ryan Cavan,
Marti Elkins Mickey Fletcher, Alayne Gobielle,
Alexander Horne, Michael Irwin, Steven Kellam,
Mari Newhard, Lydia Offord, Alan Rubenstein,
Mark Seamon, Jennie Smith, Kelly Sullivan,
and Robbie Todd.

For the world of jazz.
And for Max.

INTRODUCTION

BY BARRY SINGER

HISTORIANS CAN SUM UP AN ERA; biographers, a life. Jazz historians often attempt to do both, defining an era in terms of musical lives lived. Nothing, however, compares with the voice of someone who was present when history was being made. And very much paying attention.

Lorraine Gordon has lived more than a few lives: downtown bohemian, uptown grande dame, record business pioneer, wife, lover, mother, and finally—at a point when most women her age were just settling into grandmotherhood—owner of the most famous jazz club in the world, the Village Vanguard.

It is this last fact that casts her life with a late-blooming significance verging on inspirational. Because only after she had lived a good part of her life did Lorraine Gordon discover what she was in fact born to do.

The trajectory of her journey has been remarkable, the details, a Jackson Pollock–like swirl of fierce colors shot

1

through with luminous creative figures—not just jazz figures, but luminaries from every point on the political, social, and entertainment spectrum.

And yet, what truly distinguishes Lorraine Gordon's life story is Lorraine Gordon herself. In many ways she was just an average person with an above-average appetite for jazz—not a musician, but a fan. Her love of the music, however, has been unusually tenacious.

Ever provocative, ever the unapologetic straight shooter, Lorraine knows exactly where she's been and more or less how she got there. Her voice is indelible, her memory selectively impeccable. Her life adds up to far more than just a jazz story. Yet it also constitutes, if only by inference, pretty much the story of jazz over the past half century. It is also not solely a "woman's story." Yet it remains one of the more extraordinary and, yes, enlightening stories about one woman's life in twentieth- and twenty-first-century America.

From the very beginning, Lorraine Gordon straddled the line between convention and iconoclasm that divided and defined post–World War II American culture. That she did so as a woman operating in what remains a male-dominated, largely after-hours world illuminates that divide from a distinct and very acute angle.

A good Jewish daughter falls in love with jazz at a precocious age. Making her way to the heart of the jazz scene she so fancies, New York City, she meets and soon marries one of the music's more intriguing behind-the-scenes figures, a recent émigré from Nazi Berlin named Alfred Lion, who also happens to be the visionary founder of a record label destined to become perhaps the most important in jazz history: Blue Note Records.

The significance of Blue Note Records in the evolution of jazz cannot be overstated. The significance of Lorraine Gordon in the evolution of Blue Note Records is similarly central. She and Lion would uncompromisingly build Blue Note into one of the finest jazz record labels of its day, recording many of the music's most important artists, from established giants like Sidney Bechet to cutting-edge innovators like Thelonious Monk.

And then, an impasse. Lorraine wants to have a child. Her husband does not. This leads to divorce from Alfred Lion and marriage to Max Gordon, another visionary music character, founder and proprietor of the Village Vanguard.

The early years with Max produce two children and an utterly unique lifestyle. Officially, Lorraine retires to pursue the most traditional 1950s existence as a housewife raising her children. Yet, during this time her new husband runs both the Vanguard downtown and the city's chicest uptown cabaret, the Blue Angel, glamorous epicenter of New York City nightlife in the fifties.

Lorraine, housewife by day, turns into Mrs. Gordon of the Blue Angel and Village Vanguard by night, surrounded by the greats who frequented her husband's clubs, everyone from Miles Davis to comedy duo Nichols and May to a young Barbra Streisand.

The 1960s add a new color to the Lorraine Gordon canvas: political activism. Her cause is Women Strike for Peace, a pioneering antinuclear organization that grows into a Vietnam War protest group of such vehemence that Lorraine, in 1965, actually makes an illicit trip to Hanoi.

Still, she remains primarily a working mother. Until 1989, when everything changes.

The rebirth of Lorraine Gordon as a jazz club owner at the age of sixty-seven, in the wake of her husband Max's passing, is an extraordinary coda to a singular life. Lorraine's stewardship of the Vanguard in the decade and a half since Max Gordon's death has proven to be remarkable. The world's greatest jazz club has been preserved, and in many ways even improved upon, by her meticulous (some might say overwhelming) managerial style. Yet Lorraine remains Lorraine—ageless, tireless, peerless, merciless.

From her earliest romance with jazz as a kid, then marriage to the music's greatest record producer, through her adult years as the conjugal shadow of after-hours New York's most enterprising impresario, everything Lorraine Gordon saw and, more importantly, heard were preparing her for this.

Who could resist such a story?

"She is one no-nonsense young lady."

—Ahmet Ertegun
Chairman, Atlantic Records

Preceding page: A portrait by Francis Wolff, September 1942.

FIRST LOVE

WHERE SHOULD I START?

I loved jazz from the very beginning.

As I write these words I am still very much the owner of the Village Vanguard, the oldest and, if I do say so myself, the best damn jazz club, well . . . ever. Before me, my late-husband Max owned the Vanguard—the Vanguard was entirely Max's creation. But in his absence it has become my challenge. Together, we two Gordons have kept the place going now for over seventy years.

Our story is the story of our club.

But *my* story is another story and I can only start it one way: I loved jazz from the very beginning.

But I'd never been to 52nd Street. I was seventeen years old and living with my parents in Newark, New Jersey. When my mother said be home at twelve, I was home at twelve, no fooling around. I had boyfriends. But my heart belonged to the music.

My parents had no conception of, or interest in, music. I used to read all the French books on jazz—like Hugues Panassié and Charles Delaunay's *Hot Discography*. Jazz was studied closely by the French long before Americans bothered to. The French were the ones who started forming "hot clubs," so we did too, in Newark, New Jersey.

I collected records like a maniac—jazz and blues: Louis Armstrong, Duke Ellington. Bessie Smith, though, particularly affected me. I believe Bessie was a great feminist and didn't know it. She was ahead of her time.

I also had quite a passion for Benny Goodman. I used to think, someday when I get married, that's the kind of man I want to marry. Even though they told me he was a rat. I loved his looks. I loved his quizzical face. I loved his clarinet playing more than anything. I loved his band, his trio, and quartet records with Lionel Hampton and Gene Krupa, Teddy Wilson and Charlie Christian.

I flipped out—madly in love with Benny Goodman. Gene Krupa playing "Sing, Sing, Sing," my mother yelling at me, "Turn that radio down!" I'd put my ear to the speaker, turn it up to the highest volume to get that real feeling in my gut. I don't know why. Nobody understands why people love jazz if you're not actually a musician. I never had a piano lesson in my life, though I did dream of having piano lessons. Now my dream is, if I ever retire, I'm going to take piano lessons.

My brother, Philip, and I both listened to Ralph Berton, a disc jockey on WNYC radio, every day. Wow, did he play great records. Blue Note Records—this brand-new jazz label—I'd never heard anything like them, the most profound sounds. One record in particular featured Frankie

Newton, an obscure trumpet player's trumpet player, and his "After Hours Blues," with guitarist Teddy Bunn, bass player Johnny Williams, Meade "Lux" Lewis on piano, and the killer swing drummer "Big Sid" Catlett. Other Blue Note discs were led by the legendary New Orleans soprano saxophonist Sidney Bechet, who also jammed sublimely with Newton and his sidemen in a studio group called the Port of Harlem Seven. I'd been listening to Louis Armstrong and Bessie Smith, but Blue Note's music was totally unique to me. And I actually remember thinking at one point, Whoever made these records, he's a genius!

I went out to buy them, big twelve-inch discs, longer playing, more music than the usual 78s. Also smaller ten-inch sides. A dollar-fifty for the big ones, a dollar for the small. Beautiful labels in chartreuse and blue; so modern, so elegant.

And then one night, I'm in bed and my brother calls. He now has a girlfriend and he's out somewhere with her and I hear him say, "Get dressed, be downstairs. I got Ralph Berton in the car!"

Man, I jumped up like crazy. Because I was . . . well, attracted to Ralph Berton, just his voice on the radio. He stuttered a little. So sexy. I was such a kid. I really loved it.

I rushed downstairs. And there was my brother in my father's huge hearse, an old—what the heck was it?—a Buick or a Cadillac. Secondhand. Big. I used to drive it.

My brother's up front with his new girlfriend—his wife-to-be, actually. Philip had gone to some music seminar in East Orange, New Jersey, where Ralph Berton was speaking. And now, there was the man in Philip's backseat.

I confess I really expected to find some handsome, tall gentleman. Instead, there was this little guy, short on hair and height, with an inhalator up his nose. He had a cold. I was so shocked. I thought, This cannot be.

Off my brother drove, into New York and right to Ralph Berton's apartment down on Hudson Street in Greenwich Village—I still remember where it was; I pass the spot all the time today. Two flights of stairs led up to a cold water flat, where we sat on barrels, crates, a big bed in the living room—you know, a poor guy living the Villager life.

Ralph Berton's brother was Vic Berton, the drummer who'd played with Bix Beiderbecke. Ralph Berton knew everything about jazz. And about young girls too.

We plopped down on the bed and he began playing Louis Armstrong records, scatting along with them. And I sat there, goggle-eyed; all of a sudden he was transformed again into the gorgeous man I'd imagined. Squat. Almost bald. But gorgeous.

Was Ralph Berton interested in me? Of course he was; he'd be interested in any adorable young girl who loved jazz. We all became friends—Ralph, my brother, his wife-to-be, and me. We were there a lot after that, at Ralph Berton's apartment. But my brother's girlfriend had to be home by midnight too, so my brother left me one night at Ralph's. Silly boy. That's the kind of trusting brother I have—he left to take the girlfriend home to New Jersey and then he came back to get his sister.

Losing one's virginity is not such a big moment. Having your first period is far bigger. Ralph Berton was married, it turned out; he had a wife who was living in Mexico and a daughter, whom I actually met not long ago. But Ralph was really quite a roué in the jazz world. I didn't know this. For me, he was an experience. That's all. I wanted very much to

Me at sixteen, Surprise Lake, New Jersey, May 1939. Dig the saddle shoes.

learn how to be an adult, fast (without actually having to grow up). With Ralph Berton I took another step in my life.

I certainly wasn't in love with him. He was simply more interesting than some kid in the neighborhood. He was very persuasive and not harmful in any way. I felt safe with him. I don't think he took advantage of me. I think he was kind and wise, and that's it.

We now saw each other whenever I came to New York; we would have dinner and I would go to his flat or he would come to Newark. We'd sit on the floor all night listening to records. I never smoked pot. Not then. Not yet. I was such a purist. When I read that Louis Armstrong smoked marijuana all the time, I got on a soapbox about it, railing against pot and Louis. To me, it was a terrible thing. Terrible! I was just Miss Purity. You have no idea.

Ralph was the first person I met who had firsthand contact with the music I loved. It was Ralph who finally took me to 52nd Street—my dream. In 1939, 52nd Street was known as Swing Street. It was lined from Fifth to Sixth avenues with jazz clubs. You could hear Billie Holiday in one club, then go next door and hear Coleman Hawkins or Art Tatum or Lester Young, just stroll up and down that block and hear the greatest jazz in the world.

The names of the clubs were so colorful. The Three Deuces, the Onyx, the Famous Door. Ralph took me to the only club named for its owner, Jimmy Ryan's. Ralph had no money. I heard him say to the man at the door, "Hey, I'm Ralph Berton, let us in." All that finagling one has to do. I'm used to it now. At the Vanguard I always say, "Let 'em in, let 'em in. Don't put 'em through that embarrassment."

We sat in a banquette against the left wall at Jimmy

Ryan's. I remember there was a handsome clarinet player that night who had a big scar down his cheek; Joe Marsala was his name. Suddenly Ralph said to me, pointing across the floor: "Oh, look, there's Alfred Lion. That's Mr. Blue Note Records."

Well. I looked. And he was *good-looking*. Very debonair, in a nice way. Finely chiseled features. Charming nose. Beautiful black hair. Small, diminutive, in a way. I'm always taller than the men I've married.

"Take me over to him," I said. "I want to meet him."

So Ralph brings me over. Turns out Alfred Lion is from Germany. Left after Hitler came in. Alfred had lived in the most fashionable and intellectual part of Berlin, in Unter den Linden. Later I was so embarrassed to be with a German, I told everyone he was French.

Francis Wolff was there too, Alfred's partner at Blue Note and *my* future mother-in-law—the three of us destined to be inseparable, for better or worse. Frank had just arrived from Germany himself. Alfred came in 1937, Frank in 1939. They'd been friends in Berlin since their teens; Frank's family had been much wealthier, more bourgeois, and Frank was more of an aesthete, with a budding career as a photographer.

Before immigrating for good, Alfred had visited New York a few times, beginning in 1928, when he'd gotten the tar beaten out of him while working on the docks here. (No, I have no idea why.) Alfred had fallen in love with jazz at this time, buying many, many jazz records on subsequent visits. He'd finally left Germany with his mother in 1933, moving with his by-now-enormous record collection to Santiago, Chile. Four years later, he'd landed in New York for good.

Inspired by John Hammond's landmark "From Spirituals to Swing" concert in December 1938 at Carnegie Hall, where he'd heard the sensational boogie-woogie pianists Albert Ammons, Meade "Lux" Lewis, and Pete Johnson, Alfred had decided to start his own record label. He cut his first Blue Note Records with Ammons and Lewis just two weeks later, on January 6, 1939. Alfred pressed fifty copies of two twelve-inch 78s, one by each pianist. The records sold. Alfred was in business.

"Tell Mr. Blue Note Records how much I admire him," I said to Ralph Berton that night.

Well, sparks didn't fly. There was no lightning, there was no thunder, there was nothing except, "Nice to meet you. Yes, I love your records, they're absolutely fabulous. I've never heard better records."

Some days later, though, I got a phone call in Newark, and Alfred invited me to his office. The Lambert Brothers' building at 767 Lexington Avenue, across from Bloomingdale's at 60th Street, was Alfred's first real office, with the shipping in there and another little room with a desk and the filing cabinets, and walls and walls of records.

I don't like men with pinkie rings. Alfred, though, had a lapis lazuli pinkie ring that I quite fancied. Alfred bought his socks at Knize, a very fine, German-based haberdashery. Nobody had heard of Knize in those days, certainly not me. A suit made to order at Knize was expensive—far too expensive for Alfred. They also had their own toilette water, Knize Ten, which was all Alfred ever used. And it was beautiful. To this day, if I smell it, it makes me remember.

Alfred gave me two complete albums that afternoon containing every Blue Note record he'd brought out so far. I was thrilled.

Then he called me again. This time I invited a girlfriend of mine, Beatrice, to go with me. "Hey," I said, "you want to go into the city? I'm going to meet this special man and he's got a nice friend."

We went up to Alfred's office and he and Frank Wolff were so damn tired, but they couldn't get rid of us. "We thought you were taking us out to dinner," I said to Alfred, and he said, "Well, why don't we have dinner in?" So they took us to their place, a tiny apartment they shared on First Avenue.

Their apartment on 1133 First Avenue was a four-story walkup. It had a front room with a table, chairs, and a Pullman kitchen, a bathroom, and then another room, where they slept before one long wall covered with the most priceless jazz records you could imagine, records that Alfred had gotten out of Germany. He was smart, you see. Alfred had seen Hitler coming.

Bea and I looked at each other and then in the fridge, where there were, like, three eggs and some stale bread. Which we cooked up for *them* and served *them*! Our big night out.

Alfred had gotten his looks from his mother. I don't think he ever even mentioned his father to me. His mother was this extravagantly beautiful woman, Margarita, who'd been the toast of Berlin nightlife, a woman to whom Cartier had given jewels to wear at parties. When she gave birth to Alfred, though, in 1908, Margarita didn't know what to do with him. Eventually she put him into a boarding school. Alfred told me he had lived in the sort of boarding school where a piece of meat was kept on the edge of your plate as the last thing you saved to eat. Dickensian.

Alfred had grown up in private schools most of his life, a lonesome young boy. He was very much a bachelor when I met him. And here I come, this little Jersey gal who just loves jazz.

Sure, the records came first for me—I mean, gosh, if Alfred had been a physicist or a butcher it would have taken me a little longer to...fall. But I understood the music, so I understood him. Everything he knew, I knew. He'd never met a woman who knew as much about the music as I did, or cared as much as he did. Alfred, though, was not looking to get married. Far from it.

I invited him to Newark to meet my mother. He came and we began courting. My mother was at first stunned. Alfred was so much older than me; I mean, he was in his thirties. But he came to my house to meet my parents; at least, he met my mother. I don't know where my father was; maybe he'd left home again, who knows. My father was the playboy of the Western world.

All my jazz friends from New York came to visit our house in Newark. Roger Pryor Dodge, the dance critic—he was my best friend—he came out often. Roger had the biggest collection of Nijinsky photographs in the world—you can see the collection today at the Metropolitan Museum in New York. Roger actually gave me two huge blowups, "Afternoon of a Faun" and "Scheherazade." I was a great fan of Nijinsky's, though I never saw him dance, of course. My mother was impressed with Roger's ankles. He'd been a ballet dancer, and when he crossed his legs, my mother would say, "I've never seen such handsome ankles on a man."

My mother grew to love Alfred. And we did start seeing a lot of each other. I'd come into town, get off at Penn Station, take a subway, shuttle across town, and walk to Alfred's. Then Alfred would walk me back to the subway, late; I never stayed overnight. I took the Penn Railroad and then a bus home, traveling by myself, alone. It was no problem in those days; I had no fear. I had to be home by midnight. And I was. Alfred would walk me back to the train and say, "If you leave tonight, I will break every store window on this street."

If it wasn't for the war, Alfred and I would probably still be visiting each other. Actually that's not true. It came to the point where...well, it got a little difficult. I did start staying over occasionally. But Frank was still living there. Now Frank had to be evicted in some way. Frank also found a lady friend, by the way, but that was his life. I didn't care about it or look into it.

This is how things were in those days. If you had a boyfriend you were serious about, you didn't go live with him. You dated him, you saw him, you had weekends together, you went home and saw him again the next week. Alfred and I were on the phone all the time. We were clearly in love with each other. He didn't see any other women; I didn't see any other men or boys. We were going steady, that's what it's called. Hey, we were going steady.

Alfred got drafted in 1941. First, he was in Fort Dix, New Jersey, where I'd go to visit him; Alfred in his perfectly tailored uniform, the pants pleated down the front. Then Alfred was shipped to El Paso, Texas, and that's when he wrote me and said, "Please come here and let's get married."

So I did. In other words, I was a war bride.

Every young boy in my neighborhood had kind of been

Alfred and his bride-to-be dressed to kill, on leave in New York City.

after me. I was a dark-eyed, black-haired nineteen-year-old girl who didn't pay attention to them. I didn't want any of them. I was looking to get out of the small world and into the big world.

Was I a virgin on my wedding night? I can't lie. I disliked myself a little for having allowed myself to be captivated by Ralph Berton. It's okay now—I don't regret it. But I wish it had been Alfred.

In Texas, Alfred was stationed at William Beaumont General Hospital, in the office, a typist. My mother gave me a big farewell party at the Brook, a fabulous hall in Mill-brook, New Jersey. So fancy. She couldn't afford it, but she did it for me. A luncheon.

Then I went alone to Texas. Got on a plane, the first plane I was ever on in my life. It had propellers. The minute it took off I got airsick. All the way from Newark to El Paso—unbelievable—I was so sick. Finally, that plane landed and I was a mess. I stumbled off the plane into Alfred's arms, and I think he wanted to change his mind at that point. I had a dress with buttons down the side. I'd opened most of them because I couldn't breathe. And then they lost my luggage, so that's the dress I got married in.

We took a couple—friends of Alfred's from the hospital—and we drove to Las Cruces, New Mexico, to get married. They were our witnesses. A beautiful, small white adobe building held the justice of the peace, the police chief, the fire department, everything. The date was June 13, 1943. Alfred and I went back to the hotel for our honeymoon. And I got my period immediately. Poor Alfred! So anticlimactic.

We lived in a boarding house; if you were married, you could live off the base. A boarding house in El Paso, Texas!

Wedding day in New Mexico, June 13, 1943.

We ate our meals at one big table with a bunch of Texans. We were the only New Yorkers passing these big bowls of food around. Nobody ever talked to us.

To keep busy, I got a job in a candy factory typing invoices. Since I'm a lousy typist, everything I did was wrong. I used to shove the invoices in a drawer under my desk—the boss shouldn't see what I'd done. One day I got the dreaded Mexican disease—dysentery—bad. Alfred had to call and tell my boss that I couldn't come in to work, and my boss didn't believe Alfred. He fired me. And that was that.

The war was still young. We were just waiting for Alfred to be sent overseas. But Alfred had one very weak eye, and it got worse, because he was a typist, so bad that he became nearly blind in that one eye. Wouldn't you know it—they gave him a discharge! An honorable discharge.

Alfred was mustered out. And we took a troop train home, standing all the way, wondering, Gee, now what?

Back in New York, Frank was keeping Blue Note going, though he couldn't record any music. The beautiful chartreuse-and-blue label had turned into a blue-and-white label because Frank couldn't get the chartreuse ink anymore due to war shortages.

Alfred and I went right to 1133 First Avenue. Alfred put on his first civilian suit—gray flannel, double-breasted—I have a picture of him standing in front of the door, looking very elegant. And we went down to the Village to hunt for a new apartment because we wanted to live in the Village.

Well, we came downtown and we could have had any apartment for almost nothing. The Village was empty. We looked at this, we looked at that. We had very little money. Finally, we settled on a little flat—no, a studio, on Grove Street, 50 Grove. It was one room with four windows, two on the street side on Grove, two in the back overlooking a big roof. And it had a fireplace. That's what got me—I love fireplaces. And a little kitchen—this big; and a little bathroom—that big; and one closet. The rent was forty-five dollars a week. And that was too much for us. Our landlord's office was across the street. Mr. Gallo. I went across the street to see him and I said, "Mr. Gallo, you know my husband is a veteran and forty-five dollars is a lot." And he said, "Ah, forty-two fifty!"

And that was it. We moved into Grove Street.

Seven years later, I was divorced.

Preceding page: Bicycling in Bradley Beach on the Jersey shore with my beloved Fluffy Ruffles at my side.
Would you believe some neighbor poisoned him for going through their garbage?!

CHAPTER 2

HOT CLUB

My father was a salesman. I loved him dearly and he loved me; as a young child, I thought he was a terrific father. I didn't know any better. It's only later you learn that your parents were only people, not the idealized figures you make of them. My father was sweet to me, caring, and so was my homemaker mother, though she favored my brother just a little more, as all good Jewish mothers do, I guess. My mother and I were pals. We had a lot in common. As I grew older she was still quite young, so we were young together.

My earliest memory is standing up in my crib and shaking it like crazy. The more I shook it, the more it sounded like footsteps to me. And the more it sounded like footsteps, the more I cried. My father came in from their bedroom and pushed my crib into their room, setting it down right next to where he was sleeping. He took my little hand and held it, and suddenly everything was beautiful in the world. It was a crib incident.

My Polish royal family: Jacob and Fanny Pichinson with their brood, including my mother in the middle.

My mother's name was Rebecca Pichinson, though what the family name originally was nobody knows for sure. When that generation of immigrants came through customs, the people in charge rarely got the names straight. They shortened them or Anglicized them or just made them up. My mother's family arrived here from England. My mother was born in London. Her mother, my grandmother Fanny, was born in Poland. Theirs was a very wealthy family, as my grandmother used to tell me. Her parents owned forests, acres of forests; they were involved with woodcutting, big landowners, until the Polish equivalent of Cossacks came and killed half the family because they were Jews, including, I believe, my grandmother's parents. My grandmother escaped and eventually reached England. She would later have five children.

In London, my grandmother Fanny met a man named

28

Jacob and married him. What did he do? He ultimately left his wife and five children—that much I know he did. Such a handsome brood they were. I have a picture of them that I treasure: they look like the Russian royal family. Extraordinary how such struggling immigrants could look so elegant. Father: Jacob. Mother: Fanny. Daughters: Rebecca, Rose, and Mary. Brothers: Harry and John. I once asked my mother why her mother named two of her children Mary and John. My mother said that my grandmother just got tired of naming her kids. A friend, a nice Catholic woman, told her: "Call that one Mary," and then later, "Call that one John." So she did.

Somehow they all made it to America and ended up in Denver, Colorado, where my mother wound up meeting and dating Paul Whiteman—the future "King of Jazz," you should pardon the expression—the rotund, anything-but-swinging, Roaring Twenties bandleader who would one day commission George Gershwin to write *Rhapsody in Blue*. Whiteman's father was then dean of Denver's music schools. My grandmother did not approve of this Whiteman boy, thought he was a ne'er-do-well (my grandfather apparently did not especially mind him). My mother liked to go dancing at Illitch's Gardens with tubby Paul Whiteman. That relationship broke up, thankfully. I could have wound up looking like him.

My grandfather Pichinson left somewhere along the line; he cut out. How my grandmother raised those five kids, I don't know. I did not delve into that history; I had enough to deal with myself growing up. I know that they struggled financially, and I know that they turned up eventually in Paterson, New Jersey, where my aunt Mary—who hated her name so much she changed it to Marilyn—worked in the silk mills.

My grandmother Fanny later lived with us. Fanny also lived with my uncle John for a while in Corpus Christi, Texas—J. Pichinson, who became a powerful lawyer down there. She also lived for a time with my aunt Rose, who renamed herself Audrey.

My other grandmother—my father's mother, Jennie—was a much more independent, wonderfully untutored woman, who couldn't read English but kept up with all the latest news. I used to teach her English. By the time I knew her, she was living by herself, having come here from Russia and birthed three sons, including my father. Jennie was fabulous. I admired that woman a lot.

Sometimes we were so poor we had to live with Jennie. We traded back and forth. The terrible thing—and now I regret it so deeply—is that growing up with two grandmothers whom I loved, both of them very different women with different backgrounds, I never investigated who they were or what their families were like. There are so many blank spaces in the lives of my grandparents. These people who left those European countries, they left quick. I only know that my mother's family came from Poland, and my father's family came from Russia.

The one thing I learned from Jennie (which I loved) was how to "flick a chicken." She did that, plucked and koshered it herself, salted it in the sink. I was so fascinated as a little kid. Oooh, look at those feathers. Then there were the candles that she "davened" over. That's the only religion I ever saw in my family life—my father's mother truly being a religious woman. It was wonderful; I just loved to watch this hocus-pocus. And she made gefilte fish. All I know from Jewish food is what she cooked. I tried to emulate her in later years, at least making the gefilte fish, which is pretty easy to do. But my mother's mother, forget it—Fanny Pichinson had tea every day at four. She was sure she was British because she'd lived in London.

All of these women were left without men; all of these men left their women. I have no idea why. Jennie was actually married twice, but that history is a little hazy. I know that she got here from Russia and landed in New York. I know that her son—my father, Harry Stein—was born in New York. I know that my mother married Harry Stein when she was very young. I know that Harry changed my mother's name to Betty. No one ever made it specific how they met. At a dance, I think.

My mother could sew. She could have been a couturier; she made all of my clothes. I never wore anything from a store; everything I ever wore was made by hand or on a sewing machine—underwear, dresses, coats—I was the best dressed kid in school. My mother could make me an outfit out of a shower curtain. And she fashioned everything on me. All I remember is pins being stuck into me: "Stand there, turn, don't move."

My mother had very elegant taste; she was very sensitive and very beautiful. My father had style. It was the saint and the sinner—my mother was the saint; my father, the sinner. Two people were never more mismatched in their lives. But she liked him. Through thick and thin. And mostly it was thin. He wasn't the greatest father in the world. He loved me; he hated my brother. A typical American family.

What did he do? Everything. He was a gambler. He was the playboy of the Western world—very handsome and very tall, very big and robust. Just loved the big life, even though he couldn't afford it: white-on-white shirts, manicured nails. I would make fun of him for that. He held all kinds of jobs as a salesman, also businesses of his own—he had a lit-

My mother and father. So sharp.

tle restaurant and then a bar. The man just wanted a lot of things that he could not manage to hang on to. So my mother went to work.

I was born October 15, 1922. My brother, Philip, was born in 1919. We lived on many different streets in Newark; we moved a lot. I went to Maple Avenue Grammar School and had lots of friends. Then I went to Arts High on High Street. I really had artistic tendencies: I wanted to draw and paint. I used to model for a friend of mine who is still a friend to this day, Paul Bacon, a great artist. I was his model.

I transferred to Weequahic High School (ahead of Philip Roth by about ten years), and ultimately graduated from there. My plan was to go to Parsons or some other art-oriented school in New York. But I never had any encouragement from my mother. Though you don't need encouragement, of course; if you got it, you got it. I always thought I was going to be an artist. I was drawing from the time I could first hold a pencil. But I never was an artist and I never became an artist. I only had an art for finding these wonderful men who encouraged me in whatever way possible, with our love of jazz, our mutuality.

It was around this time, actually, that jazz came into my life. My brother and I began collecting jazz records, and we became very involved with the music. Nothing commercial; no Wayne King or any other bands that played some gooey, white bread sort of pabulum. My brother and I used to go door to door in the black neighborhoods because that's where the best records were. We'd knock on people's doors, offering them a quarter a record. And they would bring the records out to us—blues records by Ida Cox or Ma Rainey, all kinds of fantastic old music. Once my brother got a very rare

King Oliver disc that had been in a closet and a big chunk of it was missing. My brother was heartbroken. Whoever it was who gave it to him said, "Come back next week. We'll find the other piece." And they did! They moved around some junk and found it. Philip glued the pieces back together.

We then formed our nice little Hot Club. The Hot Club of Newark consisted of about ten or twelve of us. My best friend, Evelyn Dorfman, was in it; she and I were the only two women. But Evelyn died. I went to see her every day in a hospital in Caldwell, New Jersey. What is this strange thing, I'd ask her doctor, what's wrong with her? TB, he said.

Some of the Hot Club guys later were killed in the war. John Von Bergen was killed. Some of the guys are still around today. Dick Scopp is still in Jersey, Boris Kwaloff (no, not Karloff—can you believe it?) still corresponds with me. Paul Bacon and I still get together.

Our headquarters was the Neighborhood House, a two-story place—it was like the local Y. My family lived then on High Street, right on the convergence between black Newark and white Newark. The Neighborhood House was over in the black section. We would meet there—you could rent a room for perhaps a dollar a day—and everybody would have an assignment, you'd have to share what it was that you'd learned about jazz. I remember one of my assignments was Bessie Smith. I brought my records. Everybody sat around on the floor. We had a little record player and I delivered the story of Bessie Smith, complete with recorded examples. I described how terrible black life was in those days, how bad things were, the poverty that dominated the world of black people. And I played "Backwater Blues" and

"Nobody Knows You When You're Down and Out." Those songs to me were poetry—pure, pure poetry.

I got a job at a record store on Branford Place, a neat little shop called the Music Box. The owner, a nice guy named Jack Cedar, was a classical music man. I told Mr. Cedar I liked records; I didn't tell him what kind. And he hired me.

The Music Box had listening booths, like so many record shops did in that day. You could go into one and listen to a record before buying it. Mr. Cedar would leave me in charge. And here came the new shipments, which I had to put away—sometimes jazz records on the Bluebird or Victor labels, records by Duke Ellington and Jelly Roll Morton. I'd call the Newark Hot Club kids and say, "Hey, we just got some new Jelly Roll Mortons in." And they'd all come down and we'd all pile into a booth together and play the latest arrivals. Until I got fired. Mr. Cedar finally said, "That's it."

I cried. Boy, I really loved that job.

The Hot Club of Newark began to put on jam sessions. The Erteguns, among others, used to come—Nesuhi and Ahmet—later the impresarios of Atlantic Records. Who the hell were they then? Nobody. Then we met some kids from New York who loved jazz too, and we started putting on shows together, with New York jazz musicians. We had an old upright piano, and these wonderful jazzmen would come and bang on it. I recall in particular the pianists Art Hodes and Joe Sullivan. Jazz fans in those days were a passionately interlocked group. We knew who every musician was. We followed their careers so closely.

The only jazz giant I met personally as a kid was Jabbo Smith. To this day most people don't know what a great, great talent he possessed. Jabbo Smith had been groomed in Chicago in the 1920s to challenge Louis Armstrong as jazz trumpet king. Well, it didn't happen that way. Still, the records he made at that time on Brunswick prove what a tremendous artist Jabbo Smith was.

Turns out this great pioneer was living right there in

Newark, playing at a jazz club called the Alcazar. My goodness, Jabbo Smith! Right next door!

The Alcazar was a fabulous black club in the heart of Newark. It looked like nothing. You walked into a bar, a seedy bar that smelled of beer, and there was a stage up front and there was a big cutout of Louis Armstrong behind the stage. There was an upright piano, some tables and chairs; there was no other decoration, nothing like you might see in jazz clubs today. People drank, and they

The Alcazar, Newark, New Jersey, circa 1938. That's Jabbo with his trumpet, first chair on the left. Guitarist Willie Johnson is second from right. The pianist peeking over Jabbo's shoulder is the legendary Donald ("the Lamb") Lambert.

sometimes danced too, but they weren't necessarily listening to the music. We came for the music, period. Elmer Chambers, another trumpet player you wouldn't know, who was born in Newark, played at the Alcazar. Sarah Vaughan was also from Newark. Jabbo advised Sarah and helped her get to the Apollo Theater in Harlem.

We hit the Alcazar in the evening. Believe me, getting in wasn't easy. Willie Johnson, who was the Alcazar's guitar player, used to be dumbfounded: "What are you kids doing in here?" They were kind of amazed at us because we were so sweet and white and we wanted to hear Jabbo Smith. Why? Because we'd read about him and had heard his records. You love the music, you learn, you know? We learned to tell the difference between the horn playing of King Oliver, Louis Armstrong, and Jabbo Smith. I could tell.

We were groupies, though not like the kids today you see hanging around rock groups; we were really serious, dedicated solely to the music. It was serious stuff, and we treated it seriously: we read all the books on jazz; we listened to every recording ever made; we knew who the soloists were by their sound. Was that a bad way to grow up? I think it was terrific.

Why did jazz grab me? That's a very good question. And I've never been able to answer it. Certainly my parents were in no way responsible; they didn't know what the heck was going on. I'd listen to Bessie Smith singing "Empty Bed Blues," and my mother would ask, "What are you listening to?"

Was I following in my brother's footsteps? Maybe. But we were in total agreement about jazz; if he'd fallen in love with something else, I doubt I would have followed him. And then, of course, *I* fell in love with Benny Goodman. I thought he was *it* as a musician. He also had an integrated band, nearly, and that meant the world to me. As a kid, as a young girl, I went to Benny Goodman concerts in Newark at the Adams Theater and danced in the aisle, jitterbugging. Benny *sent* me.

My parents loved and trusted my brother and me. If I was with him, that was cool. My parents didn't actually know where I was most of the time. I think the Depression did hit my family hard, though I didn't notice much of a difference. No one jumped out of a window, but my father found it even tougher getting jobs. He left home many times. And we were so happy when he left. My brother and I would tell my wonderful mother, "We'll take care of you, Mommy. We're both working. You don't need him." No, no, she needed him. She couldn't wait until he came back. There was a fatal attraction there. My brother and I could not figure it out. Our mother was charming, beautiful, intelligent. She was in love with the guy—that was all.

We wanted my father out. Why? Because he was a bully ... to my mother, not to me. I could stand up to him. He was a little scared of me because I was tough as a kid. I'd demand certain behavior from him. I'd look him straight in the eye and he'd back down. I'd kind of try to control him.

It was very painful growing up in that charged atmosphere. Though there were pleasant times too, I suppose. Was the music an escape? I don't think so. You know, I also collected stamps. I was still drawing and hoping to be an artist. If I didn't have the music, though, I guess my life would have been about listening to the squabbles between my mother and father. What a lousy scene that would have been, waiting for the storm to subside. But I didn't know any different. I thought this was the way people lived.

When I was in high school, New York was beckoning, beckoning all the time. I even came into the city occasionally with my mother. All she kept saying was: "I can't take all of these *people*." It was pretty overwhelming for me too.

In the early days, Evelyn Dorfman, my friend in the Hot Club of Newark, and I would come in and ride a bus uptown to the Commodore Record Shop, the mecca of jazz in those days. I can remember riding up through downtown New York and passing all these tool companies, tools and lathes, and marveling at this whole neighborhood devoted entirely to mechanical devices. I remember thinking: That's what I like about New York; everything has its own section.

New York was kind of a fairyland of things that had no particular meaning, but were beautiful to me. I didn't think about living there, not at first. I did think about getting married. Boys had certainly discovered me, but boys from the neighborhood I was simply not interested in. My mother would say, "What's wrong with this one?" And I'd say, "Mother, no." New York men attracted me. I didn't know any, but I thought, if there are men in this world for me, they had to be New York men.

Of course, I thought about having a family. I was a very ordinary young woman in that respect. It had to be somebody special, though, I knew it wouldn't be the boy next door. I went out, I was very social, but I found no one that I wanted to pursue, at first. And I needed to be the pursuer. That was for sure.

"She's a Blue Noter forever."

—Bruce Lundvall
President/CEO, Blue Note Records

Preceding page: In the studio for a Blue Note recording session flanked by trombonist Vic Dickinson and Sidney Bechet, December 1945.

CHAPTER 3

BLUE NOTE

ALFRED NEEDED ME. We both loved the music and Alfred was so glad to have me with him. I learned how to type. I did all the bookkeeping. And though I didn't know what public relations meant, I did that too.

Every day we went to our office—it was ours now—two rooms and a desk that Alfred and I shared. I had a type-writer. We had filing cabinets. We'd sit down and open the mail. Some orders would come in, we'd be so excited. Frank would go into the room where all the records were stacked and fill orders, then take the packages to the post office, and ship them out. I would type up the invoices. The money, the checks, came in. We must have been making money, not hand over fist, but enough to support our poor lives. We paid the rent at Lexington Avenue; we paid our rent at home. We even had a little car, a Pontiac—"The *Asel*," we called it (the donkey, in German). It was the cutest thing. Alfred loved that car.

I mean, we were little people in a little business. But we were selling something fabulous.

Alfred's best-selling prewar disc had been a smoldering version of the George Gershwin classic "Summertime" recorded by Sidney Bechet, who became a great friend of Alfred's and, in time, of mine. The first sessions Alfred produced upon our return were in November and December of 1943, a pair of very important solo piano performances by James P. Johnson, one of the originators of stride piano. James P. was so extraordinary. It was like sitting before God to hear him play. The world that he came from doesn't exist anymore; he inhabited a golden age, during which, among other things, James P. wrote for Broadway the era-defining hit tune "Charleston," and gave Fats Waller his first piano lessons. He was a wonderfully gentle, huge man, with hands that were enormous. I used to sit there and watch him at recording sessions. I was thunderstruck. These musicians had been my idols. Working so closely with them was very meaningful for me.

In January 1944, Alfred brought the Edmond Hall Quintet into the studio. Hall was a New Orleans–born clarinetist who swung. Just before leaving for the war, Alfred had recorded him in a unique quartet setting with Charlie Christian, my guitar idol (playing acoustic rather than the electric guitar that he'd practically invented), along with Meade "Lux" Lewis on celesta! Very unorthodox. This time around, Hall brought along what was essentially his band at the enormously important downtown nightspot Café Society, one of the few integrated clubs in New York City at that time (along with the Village Vanguard). Hall had a superb small group that featured

At my desk at Blue Note with Frank Wolff over my shoulder (as always), March 1946.

the brilliant Red Norvo on vibes and my man Teddy Wilson on piano.

Following the Hall Quintet, Alfred recorded James P. Johnson again, but with a group of fine sidemen this time, including trumpeter Sidney DeParis, trombonist Vic Dickinson, and Ben Webster, one of the all-time titans on tenor sax. All the stories I've heard since about Ben Webster as a man with a temper when he drank—I would never have known that he could get so rough. To me, he was just very sweet and so soulful.

Alfred was clever. He scheduled most of his recording sessions late at night. This was kind of an innovation. Musicians loved to work at night, after they got through playing somewhere. It bred a very special kind of atmosphere in the studio, relaxed but focused.

Alfred at this time also recorded a handful of marvelous white jazz players: Max Kaminsky, Art Hodes. People would later call their traditional, Chicago-by-way-of–New Orleans jazz music "Dixieland," a terminology I detest and never use. They were great musicians. I loved Max Kaminsky—adorable trumpet player. Art Hodes, well, I thought he was the greatest. Today I wouldn't say so, but then I thought that his real honky-tonk style of piano playing was the end.

During Alfred's wartime absence, the Commodore Record Shop had handled distribution of Blue Note's back catalog, but they hadn't done much with it. Frank still took the orders; Commodore just shipped them. The Commodore shop carried all kinds of small labels, and Commodore's own records, of course, alongside the major jazz labels—Victor, Columbia, Decca. Commodore handled HRS, United Hot Clubs of America; there were ten to twenty small labels that put out excellent jazz recordings. Commodore sold them all. But Blue Note was the biggest, next to Commodore, so far as recording what was *happening*. The other companies were much more historical in their approach to music. Blue Note was too, at first, but Alfred soon grew far more adventurous.

Initially Alfred and I were entirely into older jazz. We agreed on the music. I mean, we recorded someone not because I said so or he said so, but because *we* said so. We'd hang out, hearing musicians, meeting them, getting to know them. The musicians knew that Alfred had this little label. One musician tells another, you go to a club, you sit down at a table, people come up to you and say, "You gotta hear this

Four jazzmen and a girl clowning around at the end of a Blue Note recording session. That's pianist Art Hodes (with the bottle), drummer Freddie Moore, Alfred, and trumpeter Max Kaminsky. You figure out the date.

guy... listen, you have to hear this singer." It's like that today still at the Vanguard; I'm so loaded down with CDs from people I don't know, but I listen.

In July 1944, Isaac Abrams Quebec, a tenor saxophonist better known around town as "Ike," cut his first record for Blue Note. Ike Quebec was a wonderful artist and a wonderful man. I listen to his records today and they make me weep. He had a thick, luscious tone, especially on ballads, and a nice forward-thinking musical mind.

Ike was called "Face"—that was his nickname. "Hey,

Face, how ya doing, man?" Musicians are terrific—they've got all kinds of names for each other. And Ike did have this big face. I was very fond of him. It was a mutual admiration that we shared. To begin with, Ike was from Newark too. I knew his wife, Kathleen. Ike and Kathleen would come to our house and listen to all the takes of our latest sessions.

I didn't get friendly with every musician we recorded. Half of them probably didn't even know that I was alive, because Alfred and I sat in the recording booth behind a glass wall. We'd discuss what numbers they wanted to play, put together ten tunes, each tune three minutes long. It's not like today, where the guys go into studios and rehearse and someone's writing this and that, and you have all kinds of arrangements. It was much freer. Jazz was looser. In these early years our musicians often just got up and blew. They knew all the blues numbers imaginable, and they seemed to improvise it all.

It was Ike Quebec who began bringing many of the newer-generation players to our attention. More and more Alfred and I were growing venturesome, and Alfred now came to rely increasingly on Ike's judgment. We started going to clubs like the Royal Roost and Birdland, on Broadway near 52nd Street, because that's where all the new young guys were playing this new music called bebop.

Alfred began to hire these younger, cutting-edge, mostly black musicians. Like Art Blakey, the master drummer from Pittsburgh, who'd just left Billy Eckstine's band and was branching out with an octet he called the Jazz Messengers. Art Blakey and Ike Quebec were good friends. I started to see Art around quite a bit; he would come to our apartment before a session or after a session and bring along a lot of other musicians. Art was a very social fellow. Most of the people he was playing with at that time were brilliant young originals whom nobody knew. Many of them had met in the Eckstine band. They all seemed to hang together in a group.

There was Tadd Dameron, a superb arranger and composer. Tadd always had a fascination with adventurous harmonies and unorthodox voicings, even during his early days writing for swing bands. Now this fascination developed into the most accomplished bebop arranging vocabulary in jazz. Tadd managed to capture the very essence of bebop with his gorgeous writing for ensembles. Rarely has a non-soloist done it more elegantly.

Tadd was one of the first bebop guys Blue Note recorded—initially as a pianist sideman behind the goofy vocalist (my pal) Babs Gonzalez in February 1947, but soon after that, in September of 1947, as leader of the Tadd Dameron Sextet, a historic session that introduced many of Tadd's signature compositions, "The Chase," "The Squirrel," "Dameronia," "Our Delight."

Tadd was a very handsome, charming man, very studious. He'd just sit down with his pen and music paper at the sessions and perfect these extraordinary arrangements, which was quite new for us.

Fats Navarro, I remember also. Fats, who was destined to die so young of tuberculosis just three years later, played the most gorgeous trumpet lines at Tadd's session. And Miles Davis. Tadd and Miles, as co-leaders, would take a group in 1949 to the Paris Jazz Festival, where they were rapturously received.

Miles, I loved. Oh, yes, I thought Miles was the wildest. I always did, except when he started dressing funny in his dotage. Miles began recording for Alfred in 1952, and we became very good friends. He was still a kid from East St. Louis, just twenty-six years old but already a veteran of Charlie Parker's first working band and an innovator in his own right as the leader on a series of then-recent Capitol recording sessions now known as *Birth of the Cool*.

We used to go out for dinner to a restaurant on Third Avenue, a fish joint called King of the Sea, where Miles would order a fish the size of the table. Then we'd go to his place. I got to know Frances, that wonderful wife of his; she was a dancer, a very sweet woman. I hung out with Miles through two husbands of my own, Alfred and then Max Gordon.

Miles was a little skinny kid when he first recorded for Alfred. He had this car, a Maserati. It was an unbelievable low-slung number—people would stop on the street and stare. One night after a dinner at King of the Sea, Miles said to me, in that gravel-and-shrapnel growl of his: "Come outside, get in there, get behind the wheel. I want to see if you can handle this."

I could drive, but, oh man! "Shift," Miles said. "Put your foot down on the clutch!" I couldn't, that clutch was so heavy.

"How do you do it?" I asked him. "You have such skinny legs." Miles just laughed. It was a powerhouse.

Miles wasn't as arrogant then as he became later on when he played for Max at the Vanguard. Yes, he was always hard on white people. Miles was not too friendly toward white folks, but I wasn't white or black or anything—I was just Alfred's wife. No musician ever treated me badly. It never occurred to me to even think about it. I mean, no musician even made a pass, except one guy, and I gave him a good smack in the face for it.

Who? Art Blakey. Oh my, he just put his hands on me, and I pushed him away. Not in the recording studio, in my *own* apartment. Art would always make remarks to me. Hey, it's not hard to make a pass at a woman. You don't have to throw her on the floor. You can say certain things just walking by. You can just do all kinds of things and make yourself known.

I liked Art's drumming a lot, but, you know, don't mess with me. I was very aloof. I wasn't looking for anybody or anything.

I know now that a lot of these men had drug habits. I really wasn't aware of it then, frankly. I guess I knew it existed, but I never saw it up close. I mean, I never saw anybody using. The most I ever witnessed was marijuana; that was the only thing that ever passed my eye, because everyone smoked pot. Louis Armstrong *lived* on pot. I used to be against it. As I said, I was standing on a soapbox insisting that Louis was going to ruin himself. I was very upset about it.

I remember being at Alfred's apartment one night, before we were married. Alfred had many friends I didn't know. He and his posse were in another room this night, the one that was filled with records, plus a record player. The door was closed. I sat alone, thinking, "Who are they? I don't like them. I'm here all the way from Newark, New Jersey."

Alfred was starting to sweat, though, I know. He kept coming out to me every few minutes, almost pleading, "Come in!"

"No, " I kept saying. "I don't know them."

Finally, a man came out of that room, a young man, and he said to me, "Have you got a comb?"

He's going to comb his hair with my comb? I thought. Still, I gave him my comb, thinking to myself, I'll throw it away afterward.

The guy had this big square of newspaper under his arm. Now he opened it up, took my comb and started removing the seeds from his marijuana stash.

I didn't know! This was the first time in my life I'd ever seen marijuana up close. "Well!" I gasped. "Alfred!" I then hollered. "Come here. I want to talk to you."

Do you know Alfred made them all leave on my account? Those cats packed their shellac and left the track. I mean, they all walked right past me to get out the door, and they all gave me dirty looks like I'll never forget.

So yes, a lot of our musicians were probably on drugs too. A lot of them. They may still be today and I don't know it. Nor do I care. That's just the way it is. I mean, these were, and still are, very serious musicians, regardless of their habits.

But, you ask, did I really never, ever smoke pot, even once?

I'll tell you. I did. And you'll never believe who introduced me to it.

How about Sidney Bechet?

Sidney visited with us a great deal in those days, coming over to cook—usually rice and beans, I mean, the real thing. He was a stately gray-haired gentleman with a tart tongue that could be more than tart on occasion. Though his abrasive personality had frequently worked against him, in terms of popularity, Sidney's creative contribution to the early evolution of jazz was in many ways as significant as Louis Armstrong's. A virtuoso instrumentalist and

At our home with Sidney Bechet and Sidney's nephew, Leonard, February 17, 1945. Oh, did I love that fireplace.

improviser, Sidney was in every way Louis's musical equal.

Like Louis, Sidney was a child of New Orleans, born—unlike Louis—into a large, musical New Orleans family. At

Choosing Blue Note session takes at home, September 1944: Alfred, me (listening so intently), Ike Quebec, Ram Ramirez, and his wife, Rosalyn.

age six or so, Sidney had borrowed his brother's clarinet and taught himself to play, in time becoming a protégé of George Baquet, one of the city's top first-generation jazz clarinetists. By the time he was nineteen, Sidney was a local prodigy, having already played in just about every important local band, alongside New Orleans jazz legends like Freddie Keppard, King Oliver, and Bunk Johnson. In 1916, he headed for Chicago. Three years later, he was in New York working with Will Marion Cook's Southern Syncopated

Orchestra. When that group toured Europe, Sidney's playing was applauded by audiences that included the conductor Ernest Ansermet, whose published assessment of Sidney's skill was perhaps the earliest critical praise offered a jazz musician by a member of the classical music establishment.

In the early 1920s, Sidney concentrated increasingly on the soprano saxophone, bringing to it the same brilliant technique and fat vibrato that his clarinet playing had. His obbligato work behind blues singers of the day was, like Armstrong's, of a quality rarely before heard in jazz.

In 1925, Sidney worked briefly for one of his greatest admirers, Duke Ellington. He then returned to Europe, performing in Paris with Josephine Baker's notorious *Revue Nègre*, before leaving on a tour of Russia that included performances in Kiev, Odessa, and Moscow. Sidney did not sail home until 1931, gigging all across Europe, with time out for an eleven-month jail sentence after he shot someone in Paris.

Back in New York, Sidney formed the New Orleans Feetwarmers, a swinging bunch, with his pal, cornetist Tommy Ladnier. A year later the group folded, knocked out by the Depression. Sidney and Ladnier soon opened a tailor shop in Harlem where jam sessions in the back room were the rule. Jazz impresario John Hammond then resurrected the Feetwarmers for his 1938 and 1939 "From Spirituals to Swing" Carnegie Hall concerts, the same concerts that helped inspire Alfred to start up Blue Note Records. In June 1939, Alfred brought Sidney into the studio, where he recorded his spectacular rendition of "Summertime."

Sidney recorded for Blue Note again and again before eventually deciding to make Paris his permanent home in the 1950s. There, what had seemed abrasive and alienating about Sidney's behavior in the U.S. was affectionately perceived by the French as the adorable orneriness of a jazz original—which Sidney really was. Though he continued to return to the States periodically, Sidney's true home became Paris, where he became a national celebrity. He died there in May 1959, still neglected in the U.S. but a hero in his adopted country.

Sidney had a boat when we knew him, and we went on it often, though we may have sailed on it only once. Mostly Sidney kept it tied to the dock while he wore a captain's hat.

Like Louis, Sidney had been smoking pot for much of his life. One night, he offered me some. Coming from Sidney, it seemed rather dignified.

I'm not sure why I accepted. I guess I was a year older by then. Or maybe Alfred said, "Just take the pot." So I took the pot.

Did I like it?

Oh, yeah.

I remember Ike Quebec came by later to play test records from some session. And I'll tell you, the music sounded different. There's no doubt about it. Plus, once the pot wore off, I remembered every note that I'd heard. It was amazing.

I don't smoke anymore. I never smoked a lot, just with Sidney. I was never in danger of becoming an addict or anything. But I did stop saying no, the way I had when I threw everybody out of Alfred's apartment.

Call it maturity, I guess.

ans 1-15-49.

January 13, 1947

Dear George,

I'm enclosing the writing on Thelonious Monk, and pictures, as well as his first release.

I put his story into my own words, as I found it difficult to do otherwise. Thelonious is extremely modest and just to give you the bare facts of his life wasn't enough. It's impossible to put the strangeness of his characteristics into writing, and believe me, he's an original.

Just for the record, he's 30 years old, has lived in New York since he was 2. He's quite tall, slender build and sports a slight goatee topped by massive gold-rimmed glasses. He's single and lives with his family on W. 63rd Street in New York. He considers it nothing to be on his feet or at the piano for a week straight, without a drop of sleep, but then makes up for it by sleeping for three days and nights, straight through. He's so loaded with ideas, that before he has time to write them down, he's thought of five others. Ninety per cent of his time is spent at the piano, anybody's piano and it takes an earthquake to pull him away from it. More gigs are coming his way now in New York as his name is becoming known to the people. (I only had him on three record shows last night.) This is off the record just now, but I understand from Teddy Hill that he may re-open Minton's again with Thelonious in the spot-light.

I hope you can do something with the writing, George. You can change it around or do whatever you want with it. I feel Thelonious is just as much a pioneer in music today as the early boys were in Jazz, and this is a good time to recognize him.

Would appreciate hearing from you, what you think of the material and if the Hot Box can use it for one issue. I would like to do all I can for Thelonious and anything you can do to help me will not go unappreciated.

Many thanks and send my best to your wife and the baby.

Sincerely,

Lorraine

Lorraine

P.S. Please let me know!!!

Preceding pages: One of my solicitation letters touting Thelonious Monk, together with my original press release. In my enthusiasm, I actually misdated this letter, which was written (to jazz critic George Hoefer) on January 13, 1948, not 1947. Still, the sentiments expressed were entirely accurate.

CHAPTER 4

MONK

IT WAS IKE QUEBEC who first took us to see Thelonious Monk. Ike didn't say about Monk, "Record him." He just said, "Come on, I want you to hear someone." Ike didn't take us to a club either, he took us to Monk's West 63rd Street apartment. And Alfred and I . . . well, we *heard* him.

Monk's room was right off the kitchen. It was a room out of Vincent van Gogh somehow—you know, ascetic: a bed (a cot, really) against the wall, a window, and an upright piano. That was it.

We all sat down on Monk's narrow bed—our legs straight out in front of us, like children. I looked up. Monk had a picture of Billie Holiday taped to his ceiling. The door closed. And Monk played, with his back to us.

He had enormous hands. Those hands almost stammered, it seemed to me, right above the keys. Where are they going to come down? I kept wondering. It was just riveting to watch.

Thelonious Monk was an enigma wrapped in a conun-
drum.

Born in Rocky Mount, North Carolina, he'd come to New
York with his family at the age of four (Monk told me two)
and had grown up in the neighborhood where we visited

Waiting for the other hand to drop. Thelonious at the piano.

him, a largely black, lower-middle-class neighborhood then called San Juan Hill, known today as the site of Lincoln Center. Schooled largely with private lessons as a pianist, Monk was something of a coddled mama's boy who evolved his own wonderfully off-center musical universe. He was already, when we met him, at the age of thirty, a much-loved figure on the bebop scene, admired by a small number of mostly young musicians who understood more or less where Monk was coming from musically and, more importantly, where he was trying to go.

To me, he seemed firstly to be a blues pianist and a stride pianist, a jazz traditionalist, really, but with this grand, almost regal perversity. Monk's note choices seemed slightly off, yet he made each choice the right note in the end through his wild sense of harmony, his fractured sense of rhythm, and his unique sense of compositional structure—all of which were completely his own, impeccable and outrageous simultaneously. There were a lot of modern musicians whom I didn't understand—they were fast and terrific but not comprehensible to me necessarily. Thelonious Monk, I understood. Always. Monk was a revelation. From our very first encounter, he was right in my groove.

He was always working on something new. That day we heard him composing what would turn out to be "Ruby, My Dear," one of Monk's most admired signature compositions. He didn't even have a title for it yet. I just loved the melody, so much so that I can remember thinking, Boy, I wish he'd name it after me—call it "Sweet Lorraine" or something. In the course of a later visit, Thelonious told me that he had now titled this piece "Ruby, My Dear." "Oh," I said to him, "who's Ruby?" "No one," Thelonious answered. "I just like the name."

That first day Alfred, Frank, and I practically said in unison, "Let's record this guy!" I mean, we had no arguments about the music ever. That was what kept us tight, that music was our binder.

Monk's first session for Blue Note was on October 15, 1947 (my birthday), followed by another session on October 24 and yet another on November 21. I was present for all of them—fourteen sides, all told. Glorious records: "Well, You Needn't," "Misterioso," "'Round About Midnight." All three sessions had Art Blakey on drums. At the first session Gene Ramey played bass, with Idrees Sulieman on trumpet, Danny Quebec West (Ike's nephew) on alto saxophone, and Billy Smith on tenor. The second, a trio session, just had Blakey and Ramey, with Blakey joined for the final session by Shahib Shihab on alto sax, George Taitt on trumpet, and Bob Paige on bass.

All three dates took place at WOR Studios, 1440 Broadway, our home studio; we did a lot of recording up there. We'd run back to our little apartment every night and listen to the playbacks from each session. Alfred and I had such a little, dinky record player, when I think of the equipment available today. But we all gathered around this little piece of furniture—I'm telling you, you picked up the top and there was the phonograph.

Did Monk's records sell at first? No, they didn't sell. I went to Harlem, and those record stores didn't want Monk or me. I'll never forget one particular owner. I can still see him and his store on Seventh Avenue and 125th Street. "He can't play, lady. What are you doing up here? The guy has two left hands."

"You just wait," I'd say. "This man's a genius—you don't know anything."

Thelonious Monk became my personal mission. I was really fighting everyone. I mean, I went huffing and puffing around with those records, and my mind was undivided. When I have something to do and want to do it, nothing fazes me. And Monk didn't faze me. I just knew the man was great.

We began to hang out with Thelonious—Alfred, Frank, and I—at Monk's family home. We met his mother, his sister, his brother-in-law. Thelonious was not married yet when we first met him. We sort of became part of the Monk family.

Thelonious was so eccentric and nonverbal. I really became his mouthpiece to the public. At one point, out of sheer enthusiasm, I wrote a letter to a newspaper I admired very much at the time called *PM*. *PM* was very hip, and I enjoyed reading it. I addressed this letter to the editor, Ralph Ingersoll, and described Monk to him as "a genius living here in the heart of New York whom nobody knows."

Well, Ingersoll caught my pitch. He called me and said that he was going to send Seymour Peck, one of his best writers, to do a feature on Monk. I said fine.

I remember picking up Seymour Peck somewhere in my car and driving him that day to Monk's apartment. When I started to get out of the car with him, though, Peck balked. "Where do you think you're going?" he said. "I do this alone."

"I don't think so," I said. "Thelonious is not that talkative. Without me, I don't think this will work."

"Don't worry about it," said Peck. And he went on in alone.

I sat outside in my car, waiting. Within five minutes, here comes Peck storming out. "There is no story there!" he shouted. "The man doesn't speak!"

"I tried to tell you," I said.

Back at work, I called Ralph Ingersoll. "Look," I said, "there certainly is a story in Thelonious Monk. A big story. But either I have to be there with him or you have to send another reporter."

"Fine," Ingersoll said. And back comes Peck. This time we go in together. The result: a huge, two-page centerfold story on Monk in *PM*.

What happened? With me there, Monk talked. I mean, Monk talked to other musicians, to Alfred, to me. He just didn't talk to strangers. *PM* took pictures of the apartment, of Monk's room right off the kitchen, and a picture of the refrigerator in the kitchen for some reason. This fridge picture actually showed up in the article, with a caption that described the fridge as dominating the apartment. Well, Thelonious's mother got very angry with me. She said that I had embarrassed them, and why did *PM* have to talk about the apartment? I said to her, "Look, Mrs. Monk. Your son is going to be very famous. This is just the beginning. You will have to get used to this." But I did have to console her.

I pretty much became Monk's chauffeur at this point. He was driving me crazy: "Drive me here, drive me there." I'd take him to Minton's, the club up in Harlem where he'd been the house piano player, where bebop, in a sense, had been perfected, if not invented. "I have to get home," I'd tell him, "I have to work tomorrow."

Did Monk ever make a pass at me? No, not really. Monk

Thelonious Monk in August 1947 outside of Minton's Playhouse, with (from left) trumpeters Howard McGhee and Roy Eldridge, and Minton's house manager, Teddy Hill.

didn't know how to. He was impassable, shall we say.

When I knew Monk, I didn't find him so unusual. I just thought, this is the way he is. We didn't give a damn whether he talked or not, so long as he played. His artistry was all. And if you accepted that, you were okay with him. Don't try to probe Monk or be cute with Monk. I just liked to see him walk into a room. He would throw his arms around me, a big bear hug and that was it. Then we were down to business. There was none of that playfulness I'd get all night long from other musicians; they'd come in, we'd horse around. Monk never did that. He walked in, hustled over to the piano with that shuffle of his. He didn't make small talk. Not his thing. But he made big talk on the piano. I accepted that.

CHAPTER 5

THE LADY WITH THE RECORDS

BLUE NOTE WAS GAINING a kind of weight in the record business. We weren't Victor and we weren't Columbia, but Blue Note was coming up very strong with new ideas and, more importantly, stars like Thelonious Monk. Monk really confirmed Blue Note's new direction. Alfred was on the ball. He'd comprehended the turn jazz had taken with the advent of bebop, and he had driven Blue Note out in front of that curve through our championing of Thelonious.

Blue Note now had customers all over the country. Not just record shops, these were major music stores in big cities that sold pianos and radios and all kinds of music. We mailed out our catalogs. They would send us little orders. We filled them.

Next came the thought, Well, hey, maybe we should go out and visit these accounts. Who was it who thought this? Me. And who did we send? Me.

I'd never been anywhere other than Texas. Now I planned my first promotional tour: Cleveland, Chicago, Milwaukee, and more. I had my record case and catalogs, and I went and stayed in hotels, solo. Luckily, I knew Nat King Cole a little bit through Babs Gonzalez, who was Nat's friend, so I looked up Nat in Chicago. He was appearing at one of the big theaters. Nat had just gotten married at that time to Marie Ellington, who wasn't too glad to see me backstage. Still, I went and talked my way in. I used a little moxie because, heck, I was alone in Chicago.

Louis Armstrong with me at Freddie Robbins's apartment, January 1946.

I was a saleswoman. People do it for all kinds of things; the Fuller Brush Man used to do it. I was the Fuller record lady for Blue Note records. I just thought it was a good idea to go out, introduce myself, and spread the word, which I did. And I got bigger orders. I got to meet people. It was a nice experience, a little scary but I did it. I stayed in lonely hotel rooms; I didn't know anybody. It didn't matter. Somehow I absorbed myself into what I had to do.

One trip I made was to Baltimore. The disc jockey Freddie Robbins—who was our closest friend—his wife Lucille's parents had a grand home in Baltimore. They were hairdressers and ran a very fancy salon on the main street with four stories above the shop, in which they lived. I stayed with them there in a wonderful room, ready to do the Baltimore scene.

They were charming people. They loved me, and I loved them . . . until the morning I walked down their highly polished stairs and for three flights fell *bonkity-bonkity-bonkity-bonk* over and over to the bottom—*bang*—where I hit a table and a vase of flowers fell over my head. It was embarrassing. I was alive, but it was a horrendous fall.

The records were fine, but my shoulder was totally out of whack. They took me to a hospital, and poor Alfred had to come and get me. I was so crestfallen. I'd failed him. I didn't ask Alfred to come until the next day because I was all strapped up, and I didn't want to worry him, seeing me that way. I even went out with my one good arm and my records to see the one good customer we had in Baltimore. I went in very high-heeled shoes, and Baltimore seemed to have a lot of railroad tracks. I remember walking over them, saying, "Don't fall, don't fall." Alfred came the next day because I couldn't deal with it anymore.

Alfred was soft-spoken, except if I got him angry. One night someone sideswiped me and hit a fender as I was out driving Monk somewhere. It was nothing serious, but when I told Alfred I'd had an accident, he looked at that car, his baby, and got hysterical.

He had an accent and he giggled a lot; he laughed. He had a charming voice, and the accent was very nice. He was a very level person, not given to extremes of any kind, except when it came to jazz. When Alfred heard the music, he would dance around. He had a nickname; the musicians called him Stompy, because Alfred used to stomp around to the beat. He loved jazz music more than anything in life. And he knew jazz music inside out. The musicians respected him for that. Sure, they thought Stompy was a little bit weird to dance around like he did, but they figured, man, he's just something else.

Alfred didn't read music. Figure this out: fellow can't play an instrument and he doesn't read music; he's a European working with African-American music that is so personal and so, shall we say, not easy to understand. And yet, Alfred Lion had a profound sensitivity to what made jazz so enduring.

He was a true perfectionist about everything, and he was usually right. We would talk about takes after each recording; we'd listen and simply pick the best. If an artist does multiple renderings of something, you choose the best one; forget the others. That's what I don't like about what these so-called archivists are doing today: they're hauling every take out of the vault; they're pulling first, second takes, third takes, fourth takes, and issuing them. Alfred would never have done that. To me, it's a sin and I resent it. We played every take, and we listened carefully, and then we chose. It was not just the creator who chose, it was the producer of the record—it was Alfred saying, "This is what I want on my label, *this* take." He had excellent taste. And we usually agreed: "Yeah, that's great! Whooeeeeeeee!" We'd go crazy. "That's it! That's the one. Let's do it!"

With Alfred on a rare walk in the country, 1946.

Alfred was very businesslike, but fair-minded. I think Blue Note was one of the few jazz record companies that paid its royalties. I did the bookkeeping, so I know. We paid whatever the rate was—two cents a record. We paid royalties like religion.

Some years ago I was in Chicago at a jazz concert and happened to bump into Tiny Grimes, the guitar player. I was crazy about Tiny Grimes's music; we'd recorded him when I was with Alfred. I didn't think he was going to remember me—this was now years later—but I introduced myself. And Tiny Grimes said to me, "Blue Note Records, they owe me money on royalties."

"They don't owe you a penny," I said. I was so mad. I let him have it! That was not the greeting I expected. First words out of his mouth. Not nice. I thought, Who would know better than I, motherfucker? Since I wrote the checks.

Alfred and I worked together every day. I got up in the morning with Alfred, I went to breakfast with Alfred, I went to work with Alfred, and I went out to dinner at night with Alfred. I was a terrible cook at that time, so we rarely ate at home. (There was a very interesting restaurant right near the office run by this woman, where the same people came in every night. The food was very good. Alfred and I had our own table. We didn't know, at first, that all the guys who ate there were gay. We just knew that this was very good, cheap food. We ate there nightly. Eventually we figured it out.)

Alfred was very happy. He had his record company. He had Frank, his buddy, helping out and also taking great photographs of the musicians for their album covers, which would later make Frank famous. And Alfred had a wife, which Alfred never expected to have. So he was not suffering. When we did come home, we'd listen to records, and then we'd go to bed, get up the next morning, have breakfast, and do it all over again. There was no social life; the only people that I was involved with were musicians. I don't ever remember going to a movie with Alfred. I swear I don't remember any movies. The musicians were wonderful—I'm not complaining about that—but we were little workaholics, the two of us. Our devotion was total and complete—to the records.

We had no friends, except for the disc jockey Freddie Robbins and his wife, Lucille. They became our best friends. We lived down the block from each other. Somehow we met—I can't remember now how. We had fun. Freddie had a convertible, and we'd go out to Jones Beach in the summer. We didn't have summerhouses in the Hamptons. We got away on a Saturday or Sunday, drove to the beach, and came back the same day.

Freddie knew nothing about jazz then, or at least very little. We educated him. I would write segments for his show about the blues. Of course, I got Freddie to play all the Blue Note records I could. Soon Freddie became a big star, not because of me, but the guy learned and met musicians. Basie even wrote that tune, "Robbins' Nest," in Freddie's honor.

It was through Freddie that I finally got to meet my greatest idol, Louis Armstrong. Freddie, by 1946, had become so important, he was in a position to actually invite Louis and his wife, Lucille, over for dinner. It was just the six of us at the Robbins' apartment, three couples gabbing away about this and that, though I remember at one point we asked Louis to autograph Freddie's piano, which he did. Louis seemed pleased to meet Alfred Lion of Blue Note Records (and his wife). I was so ecstatically happy to meet Louis that I didn't even mention the pot smoking.

Alfred and I were still little, piddly people when Freddie and Lucille were going out with Mel Torme. In time, they kind of separated from us. They got too big for Alfred and me. They had a baby, and they moved from Christopher Street.

I have pictures of Alfred holding that baby. And the Robbinses kept saying, "Why don't you two have a baby?"

And I'd say, "Alfred, why don't we have a baby?"

"We've got a baby," he'd answer, "Blue Note Records."

My mother always said, "Honey, have children when you're young. And when they grow up, you're still going to have a wonderful life. You'll still have a major part of your life ahead of you." Look, I grew up in Newark, New Jersey. Every girl out of high school got married. I was a renegade. I hightailed it to New York because I was listening to jazz records.

I'd always thought I would like to have a baby, though. Now I found myself obsessing about it until I landed in a depression. I didn't know what that was then. I'd never been depressed in my life. I was generally a very high-spirited young woman.

Alfred just wasn't ready. He was too frightened. Finally, we decided to move to Englewood, New Jersey—to save the marriage, we thought. Alfred figured it might be better for me maybe not to work so much.

I remember we were packing to leave our little apartment in the Village. I accidentally hit this bookcase and a piece of jagged glass broke off and cut me. One minute I was packing and the next minute I was crying. Alfred had to

That damn cat.

rush me to the hospital for stitches. My hand still has a big scar today.

Somehow we made it to our new little house in Englewood. It was one floor, very old, very charming, with a big backyard on Grand Avenue. I don't remember the number.

We also got a cat. Alfred loved cats. I learned to love them too. That cat was my baby. I have so many pictures of me holding that cat in my arms. I loved dogs too, but Alfred wanted a cat. So we got a cat.

I wanted a baby. But I didn't get a baby. Alfred only wanted one *after* I cut out. Too late. By then the die had been cast.

Preceding page: With my adorable mother, June 1940.

CHAPTER 6

LOVE AND LOSS

MY MOTHER WAS NOT WELL. My parents were living in Los Angeles at this time, and I had to go see her, though I stayed for just a short while. My father had a bar, a little saloon, out there. Not far from it was Ross Russell's Tempo Music Shop, his little jazz record store. Of course, I went to check it out. Ross was also making records at this time, famously, with his Dial label—he was recording Dizzy Gillespie and Charlie Parker, the virtual godfathers of bebop.

I got to know Ross. He had little stools in his store that you sat on while listening to the new records. This became my bar—I'd go sit on the stools and drink in the music. One day a man walked in and sat down next to me. Ross introduced us. "Lorraine, this is Charlie Parker." So what? I didn't even like Parker's music and kind of told him so, you know, defending Sidney Bechet against this young Turk. Thelonious Monk, I dug. It took me a while, though, to get with what it was that Bird and Diz were doing.

My mother was so ill—dying in fact. Of course, my brother came to be with her too—just out of the army. All of us crowded into my parents' little Hollywood apartment; my parents had no money and even less space. One afternoon, my brother showed up accompanied by a friend of his, also just out of the army. This fellow sat on the couch and I sat opposite him, very tight quarters. We hated each other on sight. My family kept coming and going, and we just sat there snapping at each other.

Alfred, meanwhile, was sending me telegrams: "Please come back. I need you." And I knew that he did. Finally, I packed up and went home. And we resumed our routine, he and I, our life together—the records, the records, the records. And everything was cool, more or less.

Then came a desperate call from my father: "You have to come back. Your mother. This is it."

Again I told Alfred, "I have to go." And again I caught a plane out to L.A., back to that tiny apartment. My mother was now about to go into a hospice. I walked in the door, and there was my brother, his wife, and that man again whom I'd hated on sight. This time we took one look at each other and fell head over heels in love. It was the weirdest turn of events I'd ever experienced.

He was a graduate of Harvard. Very good-looking. Highly intelligent. Like many just out of the army at that time, he was a soul in search of himself. He could not figure out what he wanted to do. But he became the biggest affair of my life. It haunts me to this day.

He was *my* man. That's all there was to it. He was everything that I thought I wanted—young girl that I still was. I was pretty stupid, if you want to know the truth. But we were so good together.

Together! All told, we were together not much more than a week or two.

What did we do? We became babysitters, for one thing—his brother and sister-in-law had a newborn baby, and we would babysit so they could go out.

Meanwhile, I went to the hospice every day, holding my mother's hand until she died with her hand in mine.

And he was there right beside me.

After she died, he and I went to Catalina for a week. My brother thought it odd. My husband wondered why I wasn't coming straight home. My mother's death affected me very deeply, of course. But I found that I was totally in love with this man. He arranged everything for our time in Catalina. We took a small boat over; it was so beautiful. We stayed in a lovely little apartment. We cooked and talked and danced at the casino every night.

And then I had to go home. Alfred was waiting for me. At the L.A. airport my lover stood there on the runway, practically right outside my window—you could do that in those days—like Bogey in *Casablanca*. That airplane was two seats across inside. I sat down by the window, next to a man. The plane took off, and I started to cry uncontrollably. Sobbing. The man next to me pulled a big handkerchief from his pocket and handed it to me. He wound up comforting me all the way back to New York. So kind. Helped me find a cab after we landed. And I never saw him again. Never even asked his name.

I returned to Alfred a broken creature. I was terribly, terribly lovesick—really, for the first time in my life. I'm telling you. It hurt.

We continued to communicate, by mail, by phone. In the Village, I walked around with nickels jammed in my pants, to step into a phone booth for some privacy, and call him whenever I caught a chance. We also had a go-between, my friend Katherine Mulholland—yes, from the Mulholland Drive Mulhollands. She was living in the Village and going to Columbia University. Katherine loved jazz. I'd met her through the pianist Ram Ramirez. She became my mail drop. Whenever he wrote to me, Katherine got the letters.

It didn't last long. *He* had the good sense to end it. Alfred was already feeling that something was quite wrong. My final communication from this great love was a Dear John letter in which he essentially told me: "I have nothing to offer you. I don't yet know what I want, where I'm going, and you're a married woman—I don't want to break up your marriage." Which was a laugh because he already had. But that was it.

Years later I went to see his brother, who worked somewhere in the clothing industry. "How is he?" I asked him.

"He got married," the brother said, "and he's miserable."

"Good," I said. I didn't even ask for his address.

"Playing the Village Vanguard is like playing inside this strange, beautiful, old instrument that all these amazing people have played before you. When I'm working there, I like to stop by in the afternoons and just sit, strumming my guitar. Once, I found myself playing Leadbelly's 'Goodnight Irene.' Lorraine came running out of the kitchen literally in tears. 'You don't know what that song means to me,' she kept saying."

—Bill Frissell
Guitarist

CHAPTER 7

MAX

I HADN'T ANY BLUE NOTE RECORDS under my arm the day I walked into the Bluebell Bakery—this homey little Fire Island joint—and spotted Max Gordon, owner of the Village Vanguard, sitting in a corner alone, eating a bun.

"Hello," I said. "You don't know me, but I'm Mrs. Alfred Lion."

Max nodded and smiled.

"I know a great musician I think you might like."

"Sit down," Max said. "Tell me about it."

"He's a pianist," I said. "Thelonious Monk. Do you know him?"

Max nodded again. Or maybe shrugged. I wasn't sure. He'd never heard of Thelonious, I knew that.

"If you could find him a week at the Vanguard, that would be ideal."

Max kept right on chewing. But I saw him look me over.

"Well," he finally said, "I just might happen to have a week in September."

Now it was my turn to smile.

Max did give Monk a week in September. Alfred was thrilled. Opening night was September 14, 1948. And nobody came. None of the so-called jazz critics. None of the so-called cognoscenti. Zilch. Alfred and I sat there in a banquette at the Vanguard, and Thelonious got up at one point, did this little dance and announced, "Now, human beings, I'm going to play . . ." whatever the song was. Max came running over to me in acute distress, "What kind of an announcement is that?"

"That's how he talks," I said.

There was almost no audience. And Max kept crying, "What did you talk me into? You trying to ruin my business? We're dying with this guy."

"No," I said, "you don't understand, Mr. Gordon, this man is a genius." Years later, I heard Max tell everybody about Thelonious Monk, the genius he hired.

The Village Vanguard had started out as Max Gordon's living room. Max practically had no place to live then. He hung out at some cafeteria in the West Village down on Sixth Avenue with a lot of poets. Max was a writer, a poet himself, a thinker, a bohemian. Max Gordon truly *was* a bohemian.

He'd grown up in Oregon, though the Gordon family originally came from Russia—Vilna (I think), Lithuania. Max was born in Lithuania. He'd landed at Ellis Island in 1908, at the age of three, with his mother, brother, and two sisters. The whole bunch of them then had reunited with the father (who'd preceded them) in Providence, Rhode

Island, before moving on to Portland, Oregon, of all places. There, Max eventually went to Reed College, which had just opened; he was one of its first graduates. He then came to New York in 1926.

Max's mother wanted him to be a lawyer, but Max didn't want to be a lawyer. He lived in a furnished room in a brownstone owned by a very kind landlord named Strunsky. Strunsky was partial to artists, and he would rent very low-cost rooms to people like Max Gordon.

Max first opened a little club—it wasn't even a club, it was a space—on Sullivan Street in 1932. The Village Fair, he called it, which lasted maybe a year. I think Max also was arrested for serving booze there without a license—this was during Prohibition. He then opened the Village Vanguard on Charles Street in February 26, 1935, before moving it in December of that year to its present location, around the corner on Seventh Avenue South, number 178.

The Vanguard was not about jazz at the beginning. Max started with poets reading their work in this big triangular basement on a bare floor, no carpeting, no banquettes, just ordinary chairs and tables, and posters on the walls, very political posters. I mean, the war in Spain was on then, and Max had a lot of friends who were in that war.

I have some of the books those poets gave to Max. But Max had no money to give them. People threw money on the floor—that's how the poets got paid. Max would sit there too and listen to the poets; that was his life—they'd all sit at the tables and argue about poetry and philosophy. It was kind of a coffee house without coffee, and no liquor license. I don't know what they drank. It was an intellectual gathering.

In time Max began to book acts, often three a night. Many proved to be high-caliber jazzmen. One of the very first, I believe, was a wonderful pianist named Clarence Profit, who would play the Vanguard with his trio again and again thereafter. Opening night found Profit on a bill with drummer Zutty Singleton, who was best known as a sideman with Louis Armstrong.

In 1935, I was twelve years old, so what the hell did I know? At sixteen, seventeen, eighteen, though, I went to the Vanguard a lot with my pals from the Newark Hot Club. I went to hear many of the folk musicians Max was partial to. Later, during what you might call our courtship days, Max would present Pete Seeger and the Weavers, perhaps the ultimate folk music act. The early Vanguard folk acts were musicians like Richard Dyer-Bennett, who would be the best man at our wedding; Burl Ives, the terrible McCarthy-era stool pigeon, who destroyed Richard's career by giving his name to the committee in the 1950s; Josh White, who was famous for being this beautiful lady-killer and wore his shirts buttoned low, long before Harry Belafonte did; and "Leadbelly," Huddie Ledbetter, who'd gone to prison for shooting a man, but got a reprieve from the governor because his singing and guitar playing, to say nothing of his songwriting, were so compelling. Leadbelly wrote "Goodnight Irene," among many others. He was quite a romantic figure to me as a teenager.

Max also featured a number of so-called calypso acts in those early years. My favorite was Enid Mosier with the Trinidad Steel Band, who danced and sang on the Vanguard's little wooden dance floor. Josephine Premice also was marvelous. Josephine was Haitian, I believe. She would wend her way out from the kitchen, through the tables, to the center of that dance floor. It was all very exotic.

Then there were the comedians, pioneers of the Vanguard's rich stand-up comedy tradition. Phil Leeds, a very funny, kind of desperate character who also played Broadway shows, was a longtime regular. Irwin Corey, of course, still plays our Vanguard anniversary parties, doing his highly political mumbo-jumbo routines.

The biggest reason my pals and I went to the Vanguard, though, was because there were jazz jam sessions in the afternoons on Sundays. You could go hear Lester Young, Ben Webster, all the greatest jazz musicians for fifty cents at the door, or something like that.

Those afternoon jazz shows were not run by Max. Not really. I don't believe he even knew all the musicians. He may have heard of them, but he did not know Lester Young in those days. A record company executive named Harry Lim, along with some other jazz insiders, organized things.

Max did feature a number of glorious female jazz singers, including Maxine Sullivan and, my personal favorite, the great Lee Wiley. There were blues singers too, like Chippie Hill.

One day in 1938, Max was sitting in his little basement, his Village Vanguard, when these three kids came down the stairs. There are variations on this story. Some say it was raining, and they just came in to get out of the rain; others say they specifically came to see Max.

"Mr. Gordon, we have a little act," they told him. "Maybe you'd like to hear it." Max never said no to anyone who wanted him to hear something—his ears were always wide open. So they got up and did their routine and he loved it. He didn't know who they were, but he thought they were just great. They were a really topical revue—"skits and songs of satire and social significance"—stuff created almost entirely for their own amusement, though they longed to break into real show business. They had a name; they called themselves the Revuers. Max hired them.

The Revuers became the greatest hit the Vanguard ever saw. Suddenly all the poets were gone. Max fixed the place up. People poured in. From that point on, you might say, the Vanguard had a point of view. The Revuers just broke it up. And who were these Revuers? They were Adolph Green, Betty Comden, John Frank, Alvin Hammer, and Judy Tuvim, who later changed her name to Judy Holliday and became quite a movie star, plus a friend who played piano for them sometimes named Leonard Bernstein.

Max took care of them. He called them "the Kids," because they were young and cute. The Kids got so big, though, they went up to work at the Rainbow Room; they left Max—gone! They never left him in their hearts; they all remained close to Max. I can remember going to dinner at Judy Holliday's apartment in the Dakota with Max in the early 1960s. She was involved then with the baritone saxophonist Gerry Mulligan. We had this wonderful dinner in this gorgeous apartment, which was in a turret of the Dakota. And Judy's mother was there. After dinner, Judy and Gerry went into the music room with Max to play something for him. And I wound up sitting on the couch with Mrs. Tuvim.

"So," she said to me from her very soul, "why couldn't Judy find a nice Jewish man like Max?"

I cracked up. She's rankled over Gerry Mulligan, the Irish

who-knows-what. I said to her, "Mrs. Tuvim, Judy can have Max. It's okay. I'll take Gerry Mulligan."

I was at a very low point when I met Max Gordon that day on Fire Island. My marriage to Alfred was in terrible shape. It was around this time that I walked out, just walked out of our house in Englewood, New Jersey.

It wasn't because I believed I *must* have children, though that may have been a part of it. We didn't even talk about children anymore. I just got bored with my life—that's what it was. I was always expecting excitement around every single corner. When I found that excitement and it wore off, well, I looked around the next corner for some more.

Max Gordon was around that corner. Max came along and yet I couldn't bear to give up Alfred. I didn't want to hurt him. Alfred loved me so intensely. I felt I was a rat, I was rotten, I was terrible. How could I do this to this man? But I didn't love Alfred anymore.

I had to get away. I didn't know where I stood or what I stood for. Max couldn't make up his mind what to do about me. I was caught between Alfred and Max, and no one could make a decision. *I* couldn't make a decision, except to get away. We were all stuck—me not wanting to hurt Alfred, Max not demanding that I be his wife, because he was not a home-breaker-upper and because he liked Alfred, you know?

It was just nice to get away from the both of them. My brother, Philip, was living with his wife in Mexico, a place called San Miguel de Allende. He said, come on down. You know, my best pal has always been my brother.

San Miguel de Allende was an artists' colony at that time. The great Mexican painter David Alfaro Siqueiros taught there. After the war, it had become a terrific place for GIs who were, or wanted to be, artists; a lot of them landed there because it had a great art school. My brother had come to San Miguel de Allende right out of the army, with his new wife.

I had a wonderful time in San Miguel. I became an artists' model, but I wouldn't take my clothes off. I was too modest. They wanted to kill me. I could have been a perfect model,

Modeling in Mexico, 1949.

but just down to my shorts and bra, that was it. They were really angry with me, those artists.

Siqueiros was a Communist. In time, he began to be harassed; problems came up in that little town. So Siqueiros left. And when Siqueiros left, my brother and his wife left too. They moved to Mexico City, and I went with them. Now I was living in Mexico City, writing to Max every day, getting letters back every day, and just letting Alfred wonder what the hell was going on.

I couldn't bear to leave him. See, I wanted both of them, actually; I was living that movie, *Jules and Jim*. Alfred loved me, I loved Alfred in a way; I loved Max in a different way. I just didn't drive over the cliff in a car.

Finally, I realized how much I missed Max. This escapism had achieved nothing but a dislocation in three lives. And so I came home; I left Mexico to an awaiting Max Gordon. My divorce from Alfred was instigated immediately. The fact that we didn't have children made it easier. No recriminations.

Max and I didn't waste any time. We married as soon as the ink was dry on my divorce—no bridesmaids, no confetti, though I did actually catch Max shedding some tears after the vows.

My *Jules and Jim* episode was ended. And just like that, I got pregnant, one-two-three. I went with Max for lunch. We were in the Village at this place called the Jumble Shop. I had to go to the bathroom, and suddenly I started throwing up. Oh, God, I thought, what did I eat?

I was so glad to be pregnant. But *Max*! Max the bachelor was thrilled. Our daughter Rebecca was born on October 20, 1950, at Lenox Hill Hospital. I was twenty-eight years old. I sat like a queen in bed with flowers and a baby in my

Max and Rebecca, January 1951.

arms, loving every minute of it. Then I went home to our apartment on East 94th Street. I had a nurse, a wonderful English woman—little, white-haired Mrs. Walls, who'd come highly recommended. She lived in with us at the beginning, shared a big bedroom with Rebecca.

And I went out to the clubs.

In order for me to see my new husband, I basically had to go out with him. Max had to work every night. Fortunately, Rebecca was a sleeper. Rebecca was always sleeping. So I stayed up late with Max.

Max had relatives who watched over the Vanguard in those days; his brother-in-law—his sister's husband—kind of covered the door while Max did the bookings. Max wasn't present every night—he couldn't be. Max Gordon had become quite the nightclub entrepreneur. He had a new club when I met him, Le Directoire on East 58th Street between Park and Lex, the site of the old Café Society Uptown. When Barney Josephson—the radically liberal owner of both Café Society Uptown and Downtown—got called in by the House Un-American Activities Committee, he'd phoned Max, who took the uptown space over after Barney found himself blacklisted.

Le Directoire was the most sumptuous club you will never again see. It didn't last long. Le Directoire was so expensive *no* one could afford to go. The place was designed by William Pahlmann, the great stage and interior designer. It had walls of woven pink, silver, and gold threads, and a stage that slid down out of the wall and out over the dance floor, then slid back up into the wall to make way for dancing.

Le Directoire opened with Kay Thompson and the Williams Brothers, and was the biggest hit in New York. Unbelievable! I must have met Max shortly after that, because by the time I got to Le Directoire, Thompson and the Williams Brothers were gone; I never saw them. The next act Max brought in was the great comedy writer Abe Burrows on piano, singing his parody songs. Abe flopped so badly that the joint closed. Not only did it close, it was auctioned off. That beautiful sliding stage sold for a hundred dollars with all the mechanisms that went with it. I bought two pieces of sculpture that were left from Café Society Uptown, two wonderful stone fish by Anton Refregier. I still have them in my apartment.

Mostly in those years, Max and I went to the Blue Angel—my new husband's primary nightclub enterprise, at 152 East 55th Street, between Third and Lexington Avenues. There were a lot of fancy spots in that neighborhood, that part of the city was the most glamorous; it was full of nightlife and people who stayed out late. There was El Morocco, but the Blue Angel was much more sophisticated than even El Morocco; El Morocco was a little more gangster-ridden. There was the Versailles—Edith Piaf sang there. And La Vie en Rose—we called it "Levine and Rose"—which was owned by Monte Proser, who, with mobster Frank Costello, also owned the Copacabana. Eartha Kitt got her start at La Vie en Rose and actually bombed there, but Max liked what he heard and, especially, I guess, what he saw of Ms. Kitt, enough to bring her to the Village Vanguard, where she really took off. Her next stop, of course, was the Blue Angel, which fit Eartha Kitt like a custom-cut gown.

The Blue Angel was exquisite. Max ran it with a man named Herbert Jacoby, a painfully French Frenchman. Herbert had been a nightclub press agent for a Paris *boîte* called Bœuf sûr le Toit (which translates as the Steer on the Roof, as if you didn't know—such a great name). Herbert had landed in New York in 1937, broke but determined to open a classy new supper club. First, though, he'd created a stylish, intimate spot out of a second-story back room above an Italian restaurant on 56th and Fifth—Le Ruban Bleu (the Blue Ribbon). Among others, Lotte Lenya had made her American nightclub debut there, after fleeing Nazi Germany.

By 1943, Herbert was ready to move up. Looking for a partner to go in with him on his high-end supper club dream, he approached Max Gordon of the Village Vanguard.

Our table at the Blue Angel.

An odder couple you'll never find. Herbert was tall, dark, and angular—a gloomy-looking Parisian with a beak of a nose—"the Prince of Darkness," they called him. Herbert knew everything about European cabaret, while Max smoked cigars and knew everything about American cabaret. Together they knew everything. And everyone. So they agreed to open the Blue Angel.

It was terribly elegant, very beautiful, the most elegant place I've ever been in—all black patent leather with white trim—designed by Stewart Chaney, a fine theatrical set designer. The building itself had once been an old carriage house. (It's gone now. They pulled it down.) There was a red carpet and a doorman, Sonny, outside, who opened the doors for all those limos and cabs at the curb. Then there was the maître d', Arturo—suave, handsome, elegant—all the women were in love with Arturo. There was a beautiful hat-check girl who took your coats, and then Arturo led you wherever you wanted to go: the front room, where there were tiny blue plaster angels on every ashtray, and you could have dinner or drinks; or through draped glass doors into the back room for the nine o'clock show, where there was bright red carpet, walls of tufted gray velour with pink rosettes, pink leather banquettes, and an adorable, surprisingly tiny stage with a plaster of Paris curtain topped by a little plaster angel. Some wag (I think it was Lenny Bruce) said it all looked like the inside of a coffin. But a lot of great people played that coffin and brought it to life.

I used to explore the Blue Angel by myself in the daytime. It was kind of a mysterious place to me. I loved to see how it worked. The ground floor held the club. The basement held the kitchen, which had huge walk-in refrigerators. Up a staircase to the second floor was Max's office, which was a rather big room. Further down that hallway was the ladies' room, the men's room, the dressing rooms, and a back stairway to the stage. The ladies' room had an attendant, of course, Mildred—Max called her "the Lady of the Doings"— she was my buddy, and in the men's room, there was George, "the Master of the Doings."

I'd sit in the kitchen and watch the chef, Joseph, chop, slice, and prepare. I could watch him work for hours. I had fleeting relationships—I can't even call them friendships—with all the people who worked there. I remember some of the waiters—Raymond and Bruno, and of course Arturo; they were all friends in a way because we saw each other every day or night. Max and I usually ate our dinner at the Blue Angel. The waiters were always so nice to me because, what the heck, I was Max's wife.

Max used to forget to introduce me to people. Herbert barely looked at me. He had his table full of boyfriends on his side of the room, and we had our table full of our friends on our side of the room. Max and Herbert were night and day, and Mutt and Jeff, size-wise. They were both Jewish—that much they had in common—though Herbert would have been the first to deny it. Still, they talked about everything together. They were partners; they were not isolated. They wanted to do what was best for the club.

Perhaps the most important thing about the Blue Angel, in retrospect, was the utter absence of racism on or off its little stage. Blue Angel audiences were always mixed audiences. New York nightlife at this time, particularly in the upper echelons, was still shockingly segregated. Max and Herbert were both unapologetically color-blind. In fact, it was probably the one quality that they shared.

It *was* Max, though, who brought in most of the Blue Angel's black performers. My head is full of names, all the greats who became stars there, black and white: Harry Belafonte, Nichols and May, Barbra Streisand, Eartha Kitt, Carol Burnett. I used to sit with the performers every night between shows at our corner banquette, just inside the door as you walked in. Some I gradually got to know better than others. Like Bobby Short, he was my dear friend to the end of his life. Bobby played piano and sang in the lounge at the Blue Angel. Nobody knew Bobby Short then; he was just that guy at the piano near the bar.

Max and Herbert auditioned new acts on Monday afternoons. I'd go down sometimes and see some poor, nervous stranger up there, singing, and those two sitting, listening. Herbert commanded a lot of the attention at the time as the Blue Angel's so-called arbiter of taste. Herbert, of course, had connections with French artists; Max obviously didn't know Le Frère Jacques, for instance, these four acrobats dressed in tights—*so* French, and I'm a Francophile. But Max often started people down at the Vanguard, got them going, and then brought them uptown. The Vanguard at this time was far more supper-club-formal in its presentation. Food was served. There were white tablecloths, and waiters in starched shirts and tuxedos. Max's programming was a good deal more adventurous then too. I remember John Carradine reading dramatic excerpts from Shakespeare, for example. Carradine would come in with his cape, gorgeous man, and just toss that cape and begin to read. In 1956, as I recall, you could have seen the future film director Paul Mazursky (then a comedian), the future award-winning poet Maya Angelou (then a folksinger with a guitar), and an unknown Johnny Mathis on one Vanguard bill. Eartha Kitt, as I said, Harry Belafonte, and Pearl Bailey broke through at the Vanguard, all within a matter of months in 1951–1952. Also Woody Allen and Lenny Bruce a bit later on—though Blue Angel audiences said no to Lenny when Max brought Lenny uptown. They almost killed Lenny Bruce at the Blue Angel. He didn't make it there.

Max was not a competitive person. He never said, "I got Carol Burnett, I got Pearl Bailey, I got Lenny Bruce. I got Mike and Elaine." He wasn't that way. Mike Nichols and Elaine May auditioned for Max through a manager named Jack Rollins. Mike's real name was Michael Igor Peschkowsky. Like Alfred Lion, he'd been born in Berlin, and his father, a Russian doctor, had also gotten his family out just ahead of the Nazis in 1939, only to die a few years later in America. Elaine was the daughter of a Yiddish stage actor named Jack Berlin. Nichols and May had met at the University of Chicago, where Mike was a broke scholarship student and Elaine was a broke nonstudent who liked to crash classes. Their instant chemistry for improvising extraordinarily droll comedy brought them to New York, where Jack Rollins quickly signed them up and delivered them over to Max. Inside of two weeks, they were literally the hottest ticket in the city.

Max put them on cold at the Blue Angel in a very packed house one night in 1957. The response was instantaneous. I always stood at the back of the house once the shows started—I never took up a seat. The night of Nichols and May's Blue Angel debut, I laughed so loud Max came over and actually shushed me. "Quiet down," he said. "The louder you laugh the more their price goes up."

I also remember Phyllis Diller slaying them at the Blue Angel before anyone knew who she was, sliding across the piano top in her leotard, talking about banging her husband, Fang. And Carol Burnett, who used to sing, "I Made a Fool of Myself Over John Foster Dulles" and bring the house down;

she was brilliant. I don't see anyone today like the young women comediennes of that time. Of course there were many superb male comics too—Jonathan Winters was perhaps my favorite, along with Tom Lehrer and Shelly Berman. The Blue Angel, however, had an exceptional variety of funny ladies—Imogene Coca, Connie Sawyer, Charlotte Rae, Bea Arthur, and Kaye Ballard—there was a whole string of women who were hilarious comics. Each one was very different. I don't think any of them were particularly political; they were just clever, sharp-witted, and terribly funny. I used to sit with Imogene Coca's husband, John Rox. I was always the person to take care of the husbands so they shouldn't sit alone.

The crowd that frequented the Blue Angel did not go to Billy Rose's Diamond Horseshoe. There were many strata of nightlife in the city then, and Blue Angel regulars were a rarified breed, very New York, mostly East Siders—smart, clever, well-dressed, and with a real knowledge of good entertainment. Plenty of gays, there were always lots of guys at the bar. Max didn't allow women alone at the bar, no pick-up scene—very strict, puritanical; no picking up at the Blue Angel bar.

"Well, why *not*?!" I always thought. If men could come in alone or in pairs and sit at the bar, why not women? I found this absurdly unfair.

Actually, a single woman *could* get in without a date if she knew Max. He had good eyesight. But it was not encouraged.

Did Max fool around?

Max? What, are you crazy? No. Not to my knowledge. Women loved Max. He was very interesting-looking when I met him, not conventionally handsome but intellectual-looking, a good talker and a great reader; Max read every-thing, particularly big Russian novels. I wouldn't marry a dummy. I needed a challenge, someone who could discuss what was going on in the world. I was always interested in what was going on.

Max did have relationships prior to marrying me. I've got letters at home from women to Max. He had a lot of women; he was a very gallant man, a very charming guy. I don't know how intense these relationships were. Max didn't give himself too easily; he was a very private person.

Did I fool around?

No, no, not at all. I didn't need all that. I mean, there were plenty of potentials, but I wasn't interested, frankly. The only two people I ever went after were my two husbands. I'm a very good girl.

Preceding page: The Gordon family.

CHAPTER 8

THE GOOD LIFE

I WANTED TWINS. Since I wanted one, why shouldn't I want two? If anything, I wanted to get it over with. And at this late date, you know, Max was no youngster.

Deborah, however, was born solo on July 26, 1952. I had a housekeeper full-time in those days; after the nurse left, I relied on a woman who stayed in and took care of both children. Rebecca hadn't stopped me from doing anything. Once, when Becca was still nearly a newborn, I'd gone out in a snowstorm, wrapped her up and went to visit my friend, Del, whose baby was the same age, three days' difference.

Max was stunned. "Where are you going?"

"I'm going down to Del's," I said, and I did. I took a cab and went. Rebecca had been an exceptionally good baby. I didn't know about the croup or all those horrors I'd heard about from other mothers. Rebecca had been very easy.

As they grew up, I would take both girls to school and back, though when Deborah was accepted into Hunter, she

117

Rebecca with Deborah, 1952.

rode the school bus. Rebecca's first school had been right around the corner, P.S. 6. Occasionally, if I couldn't get up, the woman who worked for me took them to school, which Rebecca resented very much.

After the lower grades, I transferred Rebecca to the United Nations school. She also could have gone to Hunter, but she refused to answer one of the school's entrance examination questions: "Why does a cat climb a tree?"

"Well, if you don't know, I'm really not going to tell you," Rebecca replied, and that was it for her and Hunter. Still, I was so happy I could get Rebecca into the U.N. school, which took only a certain percentage of American children, not many.

I very much believed in experiencing something outside of one's own little family universe—other children, other worlds, other places. And I've always been a supporter of the United Nations for all kinds of reasons. The U.N. school, to me, was the ideal place to send children for their education. I thought Rebecca was going to meet kids from different countries, see different customs, and learn about other cultures.

Forget it. All those kids from other countries just wanted to know what the latest American trend was in this or that. Rebecca did make friends with children from other countries. But it didn't rub off on her the way I'd imagined it would. It rubbed off on *me*. Because I was enthralled with the United Nations and the whole idea of it. I'm the one who wanted to go to school and learn different languages. And I did spend time there. As a matter of fact, I brought certain artists who were appearing at the Blue Angel to the school for assemblies. I remember bringing the Indios Tabajaras, for example, two Peruvian Indians who played guitars that they'd found, so the story goes, in the jungles of Peru, just picked them up and learned to play guitar. Los Indios Tabajaras came to the school in full regalia, incredible beaded outfits and head feathers. I walked down the streets with them and, man, we stopped traffic. They were charming. As a matter of fact, they gave me a guitar that I still have. I started to take guitar lessons, I was so excited.

Eleanor Roosevelt even came to the school on one occasion, and Rebecca stood next to her and spoke with her. I don't think Rebecca was as starry-eyed as I was, but still, that was a picture.

The U.N. school was in a very old schoolhouse on First Avenue in the 60s, an old tenement kind of building. Today the school has a very fancy home over on the East River. Back then it was a medieval kind of place. Personally, that didn't bother me.

Did Rebecca get a good education? Well, she wrote a lot in those days, a lot of poetry and stories came out of her. Of course, that might have happened at any school; if you have it in you, you do it. Rebecca today is worldly wise, or wisely worldly. Maybe the U.N. school contributed to that.

I do think it affected both girls to have a father who was such a nocturnal person. In their early years, Max would come home late at night. I was not out with him every night—I'd be asleep—but the girls would never see him in the morning, because he'd still be sleeping. One night I said to Max, "Look, I want the girls to see where you work." So I got them all dolled up in these marvelous little dresses that Max used to buy—he was very attached to the way his daughters dressed—and I marched them over to the Blue

Angel in the middle of an afternoon and sat them on bar stools. Max got behind the bar. They looked at him, he looked at them, and they said, "Well, okay, Daddy, let's see you work. What do you do?" Max mixed them up Shirley Temples. He showed them around the place, took them down to the kitchen, and really gave them a tour.

Sometimes actual celebrities would come to our house. We'd have dinners and the kids would meet them. Like the great jazz singer Jon Hendricks; we made a nice big dinner for him—just us, the family and Jon. Over dinner he recited the whole history of jazz to the children. It was very special for them.

We also had some big parties at home. Mark Rothko came, Norman Mailer, Bella Abzug, all in the same room. Rothko and Max were friends from childhood. They'd both grown up in Portland, Oregon. Their parents knew each other, and they'd both sold newspapers together as kids. These two men actually considered themselves cousins. Max was friends with Mark until the day he died. We lived around the corner from the Rothkos on 94th Street; Mark and his wife, Mel, and their daughter, Kate, lived on 95th. Whenever I had a birthday party for my children, Kate came.

Max and I had two elegant little French armchairs that we'd bought at Parke-Bernet. At one particular grown-up party, Mark Rothko sat in one of them and Bella Abzug sat in the other, and both chairs collapsed under their respective weights. Forget it, there went our French antiques. I owned a dog then, a wonderful French poodle named Count Mirabeau. Norman Mailer decided one night that he was a dog too, and he got down on the floor on all fours and started barking at Mirabeau, and Mirabeau barked back. That was our floor show.

We didn't have all that much leisure time for socializing. Mostly we entertained people at the club. We did what we could, Max and I, to make that apartment into a home for our kids. I did the cooking—for parties too. Once, I nearly sliced a finger off. Someone had given me an electric carving knife and I made a huge roast of some kind. Never having used an electric carving knife, I held it the wrong way and... don't look now.

There was a doctor in our building. I rushed down to him; he was in the middle of a birthday party for his children. He got me over to Lenox Hill Hospital, where they put many, many stitches in the finger and bandaged it, and I went back home in a sling. That's what happens when you want to be a chef and you're in a hurry and you want to get it all done now.

One night an ice cream parlor was dreamed up around our dining room table.

Max and I had friends—Michael Field, who was a concert pianist, and his wife, Frances. Michael played duo piano with a woman named Vera Appleton, Appleton and Field. But Michael hated traveling with a vengeance; he wanted to get out of that business.

So one night around our dinner table, we were all talking and I came up with, "Why don't we open an old-fashioned ice cream parlor?"

Everybody loved the idea.

Me and my big mouth.

We did extensive research. We went out to a vintage ice cream parlor on Long Island called Jahn's and studied it.

We wanted our ice cream parlor to be very authentic but with a lot of class. We hired the artist Fritz Bultman to oversee the design. Everything was custom-built, from the tiled floor to the fountain in the back room.

Maxfield's, we called it—combining the names Max and Field. Oh, Maxfield's was wonderful—right across from the Plaza Hotel, on the downtown side of 58th Street near the Paris movie theater. The cooking was done on the premises, the baking was done there, and the ice cream, of course, was made there (ninety percent butterfat!). Michael Field was a gourmet on top of everything else, and a lot of other people contributed their ideas.

It took us one year to go broke. I remember one night Max and I were in formal wear; it was the holiday season. We took a cab to the Blue Angel first and then were going on to a party. "Let's drive by Maxfield's," one of us said, "and just look in for a minute." Max had let most of the help off, he didn't anticipate there'd be any business.

We drove by and there was a line around the corner. We jumped out of that cab, me in my evening gown, Max in his tuxedo. Two waitresses were on the floor. Nobody was in the kitchen. I put on an apron and became a waitress. Max went back into the kitchen and started making sundaes. We worked all night. It was packed.

That's what we knew about business: nada. Maxfield's was so beautiful. One year and it went under. Too soon, too beautiful. All kinds of people came in. Marilyn Monroe was there once. Yes, she was sitting against the wall one day, alone, when I walked in. I didn't get crazed.

Maxfield's just didn't make it. I think an ice cream soda at that time was maybe seventy-five cents or ninety cents, yet some people complained about how expensive ours were. Unbelievable! I was sitting on one of the red velvet stools at the bar one afternoon—our huge, elegant marble bar—and two very well-dressed women walked past me. I heard one say to the other, "I just love this place, I love having lunch in the back. You know why? It's never crowded."

And I thought, uh-oh. That's not good. That's death.

I was still pregnant with Deborah when we built the house on Fire Island. Rebecca was just twenty-one months old. The girls grew up in that little house. I practically gave birth to Deborah there; I had to be ferried off Fire Island to get to the hospital. I came right back with her, newborn. I was so bound to those beautiful summer days with those beautiful children.

I didn't go back and forth; I stayed. Max came every weekend, when he could. We were a solid family then, you know, in that stage of family life. At first we rented here and there, until we began planning our own house, a dream house. We bought the land. Ocean Beach was too congested, so we went to the next community, Sea View, which was much less developed. We had our choice of all kinds of land, and we chose five lots, right in back of a dune because you didn't want to be right on the ocean—it was too perilous. There was no insurance you could get to cover it.

Our five lots cost us $1,650, total, as I recall.

We hired an architect. The house we built was the first modern structure in Sea View, a community of very few houses at the time. Ours had a flat roof and a singularly modern exterior, not your typical shingle beach house. It had three bedrooms, two baths, and an indoor screened-in solarium. There was no basement; the place was built on stilts, with no heating system. It was strictly a summer-house, right near the beach.

In 1956, Adlai Stevenson was running for president. I'd made a friend named Joyce—our kids all grew up together on Fire Island. Joyce and I organized a Stevenson fund-raiser; we decided we would collect things and have a huge auction for Stevenson. She and I went around with our little wagons (no cars allowed on Fire Island), collecting mer-chandise. Anyone who didn't donate anything had to give us a bottle of vodka so we could serve screwdrivers.

My party-planning friend Joyce and me on Fire Island, July 1957.

That event was huge. Everyone got so plastered. John Henry Faulk—this blacklisted radio personality (you're much too young to remember him)—was the auctioneer and he fell off the podium.

We collected such incredible stuff: furs from Maximilian's, fabrics, jewelry—we had so much that we couldn't auction it all at once. We kept the auction going for days, and the vodka flowing.

I really worked a lot that summer. Languid as I was, lying on the beach, I worked.

At some point I decided that our apartment on East 94th Street was getting a little small. It really wasn't. Today it would be great to have it, but in my foggy thinking I determined we needed something bigger. I never asked, does Max have the money for this? He didn't say no, so I assumed everything was cool. Max was agreeable.

We looked at a lot of places. We also began planning a trip to Europe. I was very excited: Max taking me on my first trip to Europe. In the turmoil of looking for apartments and getting ready to leave, somehow we almost wound up living on Central Park West. Max had friends in that beautiful building, the El Dorado, but I realized it wasn't for me. "Where do you go shopping?" I asked them. There was no grocery market, you had to walk a huge, long block. Don't be silly.

Then I learned that Max had already signed a two-year lease at the El Dorado without telling me. I never wanted that apartment. It was immense, that's true, but so what. I hated it.

I had a friend who lived on the West Side. The man who owned her apartment building, she said, owned another apartment building on the East Side. "Call him," she said, so I called and, yes, he did have this apartment on East 79th Street and he'd love to have me come look at it.

Well, I went and looked. I didn't even tell Max. I rushed over to 79th, right on the corner of Lexington Avenue, a big, beautiful, old apartment house, and headed up to the tenth floor. Nice people opened the door. And there I saw this seven-room apartment with a forty-foot living room, a fireplace, three bedrooms, a maid's room, many bathrooms, and a huge kitchen—all furnished in terrible taste. Didn't matter. I took one look and knew.

I called Max. "Get over here immediately," I said. "I want you to see this."

"What do you mean?" he said. "We've signed a lease."

"*You* signed a lease," I said. "*I* didn't. I want this apartment."

He came and looked. You know, Max was very, what shall I say, unemotional; he didn't show much. Not like me. I was jumping up and down.

"I am not going to the West Side," I said. "I hate it. No way."

So we met with the landlord. We went across the street to Schrafft's (my favorite place, I took my kids there all the time; so sweet, the imported Irish waitresses, I loved them). We went to Schrafft's and we talked.

"Oh, I want you to have this apartment," said the landlord.

It was a rental—almost everything was a rental then; there were not many co-ops. It wasn't much rent, though, by today's standards. I don't want to mention the amount, because I don't want to remember.

"Thanks," we said. "We'd love to have it."

"Fine," said the landlord. "Only, what about your other apartment?"

"We'll put it back on the market," I said.

"Right," Max said.

And the landlord said, "Good, and that'll be one thousand dollars to me."

Well, that was like ten thousand dollars in those days. Max blanched. I kicked Max under the table. *Give it to him!* And he did.

Now we had to deal with the El Dorado apartment. Which meant dealing with the worst landlords in the world, the *worst*. They were notorious—they'd been in the newspapers many times.

"We're not taking the apartment," we told them.

"You're responsible for the rent," they said.

Well, what could we do?

"Put it back on the market," we said.

And they did.

Off we went to Europe. When we came back the apartment was still not rented, and it didn't rent for a couple of months after that. Max paid the rent on both places. Had to. When a woman finally did take the El Dorado apartment, she thought Max was the super and kept calling us to say, this outlet doesn't work, that outlet doesn't work. We always seemed to be in bed when she called.

Europe, for me, would be an eye-opener. Sometime before, I'd talked Max into taking a week's cruise to Nassau, just for practice, and to get him out of the clubs. It wasn't that he worked so hard; it's that the hours were very draining. I convinced Max to get on a ship; I thought that was the only way he wouldn't be near a telephone.

We'd never been on a cruise, either of us. Friends came to

On our first cruise, to Nassau. That's the dress I went bottom's up in. Different shoes.

send us off with flowers and champagne. I said, "Where do you think we're going, Europe? We're only going to Nassau for a week!"

Our stateroom was so elegant. And Nassau was great—we

loved it. On the way home we were invited to sit with the captain for the final night. I wore a beautiful green and red chiffon dress, with red satin pumps—all dressed up for Captain's Night.

We walked into the dining room. Everyone was seated. The boat gave a tremendous lurch, and I fell on my back, with my legs straight up in the air, my skirt up to here. Max and this man and woman rushed to pick me up. I was so embarrassed.

"How are you? How are you?" the man (not Max) kept asking.

And the woman said to me, "Darling, where did you get those shoes?"

They became our friends. Rosemary and Charles Langton, who had come from England to visit Nassau—*their* colony. They were planning to stop in New York for a couple of days at the Waldorf-Astoria on their way back to England.

Max invited them to come to the Blue Angel, which wasn't far from the Waldorf. We gave them careful instructions.

Max and I got all dressed up once again that night to wait for our new friends to join us at the Blue Angel. And that's what we did, we waited and we waited and we waited. Finally, we got hungry. So we ate. No sooner did we finish than the Langtons walked in. They'd gotten lost or something. We were cool. We just ordered dinner again.

The Langtons went back to London and she sent me the most beautiful cashmere sweater with a note saying, "When you come to London—if you ever do—please look us up."

Now we were going. I wrote and told them so, and where we'd be staying. Max had a terrifically competent woman who did our itinerary. We had a red-carpet trip, all the best hotels. In London we would be at Grosvenor House.

When we arrived, Max just went to the room and went to sleep. I said, Hey, man, good-bye, I'm leaving. I went out. I had to smell London.

I will never forget that first night, walking the streets by myself with those wonderful street lamps and the fog. True fog. I'd never been in such fog. It was excellent fog. So beautiful. I was looking for Sir Arthur Conan Doyle whenever I turned a corner.

Waiting for us at Grosvenor House was a big message from Rosemary and Charles Langton: "You're going with us to the theater. Laurence Olivier will be in *Rhinoceros*, and then we're going to go here, and then you'll come out to the country to our house. We'll pick you up."

They took over. London with the Langtons was divine. They lived in a glorious house in the countryside. We spent days and nights with these two wonderful people, drinking Black Velvets in every pub in the vicinity. Then we left them. We kissed, vowed to stay in touch, and went on to Paris, where we stayed on the Left Bank at the Hôtel Montalembert, which today is very famous. It was just a cute little place then. Today I read about it and say, Gee, I stayed *there*.

Max wanted me to have something from Dior. And I wanted something from Dior. So we went to Dior in Paris, where I first encountered anti-Semitism, or anti-Americanism, I should say, or maybe merely French style.

Dior had *la directresse*, who sat at the desk and checked you out when you came in. *La directresse* looked at us like Max was some gangster and I was his moll. She gave us a once-over and said, "There. Over there."

There was a rack. I picked up a black dress from *there* and this lady was just so nasty. I said, "I want to try it on."

"There," she said, "over there."

I tried it on. It fit. But there was no belt. "Could you get me a belt?" I asked. I tried to give her some nasty right back, just a little bit, but I didn't manage much.

We did buy that dress. Very chic. Wasn't made to order, but still and all, it was a Dior. I still have it too. It itches. Itchy wool.

Through Herbert Jacoby, I assume, Max knew the big

Rome: Out and about with Josephine Premice (on Max's right) and her husband (on my left), July 1960.

fromages at the Folies Bergere. They sent a limo and brought us to the club, where we were wined and dined again. I adored it. Up to the top of the Eiffel Tower; we did the tourist thing, and I loved every minute—the food, the French. Where had I been—you know? It was my sentimental education.

From Paris, we went to Italy, to Rome. Now we didn't know anyone in Rome that I could think of and we didn't know Italian either. So we went walking. I said, "Hey, there's Harry's Bar. Let's go in there."

It was daytime. Max and I walked down the stairs and sat at the empty bar. There was a bartender, a black gentleman. Some men came running down the stairs and asked this bartender, "Is Josephine Premice playing here?"

"She doesn't play here," the bartender replied. "She comes here as a guest."

I looked at Max. Josephine Premice! Josephine Premice had worked for Max. She was his old friend, a wonderful dancer and singer. So I said to the bartender, after the men left, I said, "Excuse me, we'd like to get in touch with Josephine Premice."

"Well, I can't give you her number," he said. "Would you like to leave me your name?"

We did. Max wrote a note, saying, "We're staying at the Hassler Hotel, Josephine, and we'd love to see you. Max Gordon." He handed the note to the bartender, who read it.

"Max Gordon!" he exclaimed. "Max, I'm Archie Savage. I used to work for you."

It happened wherever we went. It was always "Max, Max, Max, I used to work for you."

Archie had been a very fine dancer. He now saw to it that

Josephine got our note. Five minutes later, Josephine phoned to invite us to her palazzo. She'd married a very rich American. We wound up going all over Rome with her and we had a ball, just because of Max's connections, which he didn't even exploit. *I* did. Because Max would have just sat there and said nothing.

Max had some shoes handmade by an Italian boot-maker while we were in Rome. They measured him and later mailed the shoes to us in New York. The shoes were beautiful. But they proved a little too short on Max, he couldn't wear them. What did he do? He gave them to Miles Davis, and Miles wore them and loved them. They were perfect.

That was a glorious trip. I've been back to Europe many times since, but I guess the first time is the best for everything. Max, on the other hand, insisted it wasn't so great. "Not for you maybe," I said, "but for me, it was wonderful."

Obviously, I didn't ask Max about money. I had a car, a housekeeper, two children in private schools. I didn't balance the checkbook. I gave Max no advice, and he didn't tell me anything. I mean, people today ask me all the time, "How's business?" I never once said to Max, "How's business?" I don't know, it just didn't seem to be necessary. We weren't struggling; we were doing very well.

Did I keep up with Blue Note Records and Alfred Lion? Absolutely. As a friend. Alfred and I maintained our own very cordial friendship. He always sent me his latest releases. Oh yes, I still had my jazz records at home. It was still my lifeblood.

I was so happy in our new apartment. We furnished it, and how! Max and I went to Parke-Bernet every Saturday afternoon. We went to antique stores. I was into French,

Louis XVI, and Max was into anything he liked. It was fine. Max got caught up in bidding—you know, he'd never gone to auctions before. I took him to these places because I loved auctions, just loved them. Parke-Bernet is gone now, but it was a Saturday ritual for us, even if we didn't buy anything. It was a wonderful museum of fabulous things.

Yep, that apartment was worth everything to me. We were in that apartment for many, many years. My kids grew up there. We all loved it.

Well, I don't know if they loved it. I did most of the loving. But I was floating high on a cloud there. What did I know from money? Or bankruptcy.

"I just love her politics."

—Charlie Haden
Bass player and founder of
the Liberation Music Orchestra

COCKTAILS
OPEN ALL NIGHT
5TH AVE. PARADE COMM. MARCH FOR PEACE!
MR. PRESIDENT: ESCALATION IS THE ROAD TO WORLD WAR III!

CHAPTER 9

WORK

ATOMIC NUCLEAR TESTING was taking place in the United States and the Soviet Union. And I had children. Back in 1955, I'd taken the kids to the park one afternoon and had been sitting on a bench with all the other mothers, when I happened inadvertently to meet this man. He was a doctor. He and I had begun talking about some kind of organization that he was trying to put together called Stop Atomic/Nuclear Explosions, which eventually would come to be known as SANE. It wasn't SANE yet, this doctor was just then playing with the notion. I got very interested, though, and eventually did join SANE once it officially started up in 1957 as the Committee for a Sane Nuclear Policy.

Now, in 1961, a flier came into my hands announcing a demonstration against nuclear weapons on November 1 at Dag Hammarskjöld Plaza near the United Nations.

There, at that little plaza with the wonderful quotation carved in stone—"They shall beat their swords into plowshares"—I discovered a lot of women, all strangers to me, women I'd never seen before. Some of them clearly knew each other. There was only one person I could say that I even knew about—Bella Abzug. She was there.

Flowers for peace at the United Nations. That's me with Soviet ambassador Dobrynin (second from left) and Soviet diplomat Semyon Tsarapkin.

Well, I marched around with them. They passed out fliers and banners; they were very well prepared. Someone said we were marching to the Soviet mission and then on to the U.S. mission. We walked; we marched. And then I went home.

That flier had a phone number on it belonging to a woman in Washington, D.C. I remember being at the Vanguard later that night and going to the phone in the bar to call that number. The woman answered. She had a very British accent. Her husband was with the British embassy—they were living in Washington. Her name was Dagmar Wilson.

I said to her, "I have your flier and I want to do something. I want to help. I like what you say here. It's important to me."

She was so lovely on the phone. We established an immediate rapport. Dagmar told me to call any time, I'll send you this or that to read. I was so impressed with her and her cry to women—to *mothers*—to get out there, something is wrong in this world, do something about it! Dagmar really got me started. That little march I went to eventually became a huge grassroots movement of more than two thousand five hundred called Women Strike for Peace. And I was very involved in it. I wound up handling all of the New York press relations, as well as marching, and I hosted meetings galore. If you ask me, did I have a job in those days? Yes, I had a job, nonpaying. My kitchen was an office where women came to organize.

We all became very involved because we now understood what was going on with atomic testing. We knew that the air was being polluted. We knew that there was cesium 131 in the soil. We knew about strontium 90. I read all the reports. I had all these magazines and pamphlets on what nuclear testing does to the atmosphere: how it falls to the ground and the cows eat the grass and then you wind up serving the cow's milk to your children. You know, the whole chain became very clear to me.

I began to travel a lot for the movement. I went to Geneva in 1963 for a disarmament conference. We had petitions, thousands of petitions drawn from women all over the world. A large group of us went to these nuclear disarmament meetings between the Russians and the Americans. We sat in a huge room in Geneva with our petitions and piled them all in front of these two men who had each other in a hammerlock over which of their countries possessed the most nuclear weapons. The American was Arthur Dean. Valerian Zorin was the Russian. We told them both to cool out.

We were forever demonstrating in Washington. I went to the White House in 1962. We lobbied our senators wearing mink coats with handcuffs hidden underneath. We locked ourselves to the gates of the Capitol building and got arrested. (At least some of us did. Not me, darn it. I tried.) We did all the activist things that Americans are supposed to do to influence their so-called leaders.

We were middle- and upper-middle-class women. Black women, working women, they were fighting their own battle. We all had fancy clothes; many of the ladies had houses out in the suburbs somewhere. We were very middle-class, obviously, but we cared.

We decided Women Strike for Peace should never be a formal, money-collecting organization. There were no dues. If someone wanted to contribute, they contributed. One woman, whose husband was in real estate, donated an

Clarifying a few things for CBS-television at a Vietnam War demonstration, March 1967.

office on Lexington Avenue, where I worked for years. I was a volunteer. Everyone was a volunteer.

More and more bombs were tested. Things got more and more frightening. We tried everything we could to make our voices heard.

Which brings me to Barbra Streisand.

Wait. The segue is not quite so bizarre as it seems.

As the story goes, Miles Davis was playing at the Vanguard. And one afternoon—this was still the era of Sunday matinees—Max asked Miles if he would accompany this new girl singer Max had brought in just for a tryout. And Miles said, in his inimitable, charming way, "I don't play behind no girl singers." And he didn't.

That girl singer was Barbra Streisand. Barbra did sing at the Vanguard. Without Miles. She'd been singing off and on in the Village at a club on Eighth Street called the Bon Soir. Barbra was a shy one. Nineteen years old. She wasn't a seasoned performer—she was new. Max took a chance on her. In fact, Max was a very generous man to Barbra early on, giving her gigs. He more than sensed what sort of talent she had. That's why Max Gordon was Max Gordon.

Eventually he brought Barbra uptown to the Blue Angel. This would have been July 1961. That's when I got to know her. We would sit together between shows and talk. She was always alone, it seemed to me. Got up to sing in a very inconspicuous dress, kind of a muumuu, one of those long things. And, I don't know why, I have this sense that she was barefoot. Maybe she was. But she had the look of a young girl. Coltish. Not dressed to kill, no sequins—you know, most people who worked at the Blue Angel, especially the singers, they *dressed*. Barbra was very plain and simple.

Until she opened her mouth. Then she was transformed. Suddenly you were in the presence of this extravagantly talented woman who could give you chills just by singing. There was nothing Barbra couldn't do with her voice—she had such control, top to bottom. And she had the brains, the good sense, to pick fabulous material—each song that she sang had a different character. And she imbued them all with an emotional core of true feeling and a point of view that was altogether unique.

Barbra wasn't a jazz singer, though she could do that. She had the chops, and if it was a jazz number, yeah, she could heat it up, but she didn't particularly want to be a jazz singer. She was just a natural. No great beauty. Which everyone was telling her, of course; maybe she was even feeling it herself. Poor kid didn't get much support from her family. Plus, she looked the way she did. But her voice was so beautiful it transformed her when she sang. Audiences were simply mesmerized. And I think Barbra knew damn well what she had going for her.

She dressed in a very original way, an original thinker with unusual taste. She bought unusual things; she does to this day.

Turns out Barbra was a thrift shop addict. So was I. The Blue Angel was near all the thrift shops up and down Third Avenue. Barbra would come early into the club with big hat boxes filled with the things she'd picked up in the thrift shops; it could be fabric, or it could be lace. She would open the boxes and we'd go through whatever stuff she'd found.

I also began to do a lot of talking about Women Strike for Peace. We'd sit there and I'd try to enlist Barbra in the peace movement. And she was interested.

Somehow, I also knew Mike Wallace at this time. I managed to interest Mike Wallace in having the woman I called "my leader," Dagmar Wilson, who'd started the movement, on his television show. Not *60 Minutes*, of course, this was much earlier, this was a local show Mike had in New York called *P.M. East*. Mike then asked me to join Dagmar on the show, and I kind of said, sort of to sweeten the pot, would you like this young singer to come on too, this Barbra Streisand?

Well, he was more than interested. Apparently he'd heard her and knew she was terrific. In fact, I sometimes think he let me get Dagmar on, because he really wanted Barbra. I was so committed to the peace movement, I didn't care. Just so long as the word got out.

We did the show. Mike introduced us; Dagmar and I, we talked about our peace movement, and then Mike turned to Barbra. "You're involved in this, too?" he asked. And Barbra

Barbra Streisand helps me hand out antinuclear petitions on a Park Avenue street corner in 1961.

replied—I'll never forget it—"Oh yeah, we're like a bunch of lemmings. We all follow each other and jump off the cliff."

Was I mad! What kind of stupid remark is that?! I almost said. I think she was just trying to be cute, but I sure was unhappy. I gave her such a kick under the table.

Barbra did in fact become active in Women Strike for Peace. I showed her those scientific reports about strontium 90 and cesium 131. She got the message.

We also talked about men. Barbra was looking for a guy to be with (this was long before Eliott Gould). I never actually fixed her up with anybody, though once she thought I did. This particular occasion, when I went up to see her I brought along this boy, the son of writer and critic Dwight McDonald, who also was very involved in the peace movement. The kid simply was with me. I can't even recall why.

We came, I did whatever it was I had come to do, said what I had to say, and left. But soon my phone was ringing and it was Cis Corman, Barbra's best friend to this day, who'd been with us at Barbra's earlier. And Cis starts in with, "Boy, that guy did not make the grade in any way." And I was dumbfounded. I'd had no ulterior motive whatsoever in bringing him along. That's the only time I can think of when Barbra turned down someone I didn't even bring to be turned up.

Barbra was terrific. She cared and she was smart. She and I went out on street corners, stopping people with our anti-nuclear petitions to sign. We had meetings. I introduced her to others in the movement. And then she went off. She got cast in a show, *I Can Get It for You Wholesale*, and, man, that was it. She was gone.

Preceding page: The head of the North Vietnamese mission to the Soviet Union in Moscow. Charming man. With Mary Clarke on the left and Olga, our interpreter. May 29, 1965. That's the itchy Dior dress I'm wearing.

CHAPTER 10

HANOI HOP

I REMEMBER I WAS HOME mopping my kitchen floor and getting very depressed, looking out the window at a beautiful town house across East 79th Street, where one of the delegates to the United Nations, Marietta Tree, lived. Marietta was a friend. I'd been to her home many times. We'd met while campaigning for Adlai Stevenson. Once I'd brought Bobby Short there for a fund-raising party. Bobby had loved Marietta's mansion, particularly the two enormous blackamoor statues at the entrance. I'd promised to inform him if they were ever for sale.

Anyway, the phone rang, I put down my mop and thought, Now what?

It was a call from the Russian embassy. "Had I received an invitation?" they asked.

"No," I said.

"Well," they said, "you will." And I did.

The occasion? Nothing less than the Soviet Union's twentieth-anniversary celebration of the end of the Second World War. I was invited to travel to Moscow as their guest, along with two other women—one from California, Mary Clarke, and another wonderful lady, the wife of the Nobel Peace Prize winner Linus Pauling, Ava Helen Pauling.

I called Mary Clarke immediately in California.

"Do you want to go?" I asked her.

"I am going," Mary said.

"I don't know," I said. "I have two children and a husband who doesn't know how to take care of kids too well."

It was an opportunity, though, that I didn't want to pass up, the kind of experience that has propelled me through my entire life. Ava Helen Pauling could not make it. But Mary Clarke was going. And, I decided, so was I.

It was at this point that Women Strike for Peace weighed in. There was a group of North Vietnamese women we had made contact with, who were looking to end the war. Let's stretch this visit a little further, we all now said. Let's see if Mary and Lorraine can get to North Vietnam.

War was all over the headlines. You couldn't eat, sleep, or drink without reading about the Vietnam War. And, of course, we in Women Strike for Peace were against it. Half of America was against it. Slowly we'd found ourselves thrust into protesting the war, a cause we certainly weren't looking for, but something we realized that we had to do. You can't just sit there.

Many strategy sessions were now held. How could Mary and I make it clear that we were going to North Vietnam solely for the purpose of peace? What were the points we wanted to stress? How could we try to end this war without aggravating our own country too much?

Mary Clarke and I arrived at the Moscow airport just in time for May Day on May 6, 1965, and were taken to the Moskva Hotel, which was old and fabulous. We had a piano in our room, caviar for breakfast. Are you kidding? It was great. We had a ball.

We knew that the Russian people were struggling. The woman operating the hotel elevator asked me if I had a lipstick I could give her, which I did. I'd brought things with me—stockings and such—just to give away. Yes, there we were, wined and dined and entertained in this Communist country, while everyone around us was having a very hard time.

I approached a Russian friend, Madame Kimatch, about our Vietnam plans. Madame Kimatch actually had been responsible for my invitation to this bash. She was attached to the Soviet mission in New York—a delegate to the United Nations.

I knew that there was no formal North Vietnamese embassy in Moscow, but that there was a mission from North Vietnam. That's where I wanted to go, to see the head of the North Vietnamese mission to the Soviet Union. I asked Madame Kimatch to present our proposition to him.

Well, Madame Kimatch was reluctant. This, after all, was not why we were in the Soviet Union. I didn't blame her for feeling a little uneasy. Ultimately, though, she did pave the way.

Even then, we still could not get past the front door. Two American women looking to meet the North Vietnamese in Moscow? We explained that we were on a mission of peace and solidarity. The guards looked at us very skeptically.

It took a couple of visits, but finally we were allowed

inside, where we met with the most charming man. Nothing happened, but he was lovely. He was also suspicious. He took us into his office and quizzed us. In the end, though, he chose to believe us. I mean, you had to believe us—we were so straight. We were not hippies, we were two middle-class American women—mothers! How could we possibly be spies?

While these very delicate, very back-channel negotiations slowly progressed, Mary and I partook in the festivities to which we'd officially been invited. We met delegates from all over the world, many of them soldiers and heroes.

Me and some Russian general.

There were generals from Siberia; there were generals from France and England. Every nation except the United States was present. Mary and I were the only Americans in town. We represented our country, whether America liked it or not.

I met all kinds of beautiful men. One of them was Italian. We remained friends for a long time. He was a fighter from Italy; he had scars—and medals. He was an important fellow. We just looked at each other, made eye contact in a restaurant, there in the hotel. Mary and I did eat in the hotel restaurant often, and, you know, you can't help looking. Well, at least I can't.

Word finally came from the North Vietnamese. We would be granted access to meet with the women in North Vietnam. Getting there, however, was entirely our problem. In order to reach North Vietnam, we would have to fly through China. That would be the first leg of our trip. And so it was arranged.

But suddenly I found myself with second thoughts. My kids, my two girls. I'd already been away from them far too long. "Look," I said to Mary Clarke, "I don't think I can make this trip."

"Oh," she said, "come on, you've got to."

I swallowed. I said to myself, "Lorraine, you do have to do this. This is more important. They'll grow up fine. They'll understand later. Someday they'll be proud of their mother."

First, we went to Irkutsk in Siberia, where we stayed overnight. It was beautiful. Siberia may be cold and forbidding, but the day I was there it was very warm and little girls were all around us, staring curiously. Then a plane with propellers took us into China. At the airport I remember thinking, China! What am I doing in China?

We landed in Beijing, where we were met by a translator and taken to the Friendship Hotel. Over the course of two days, we toured quite a bit, even visited the Forbidden City, where I stood in my high-heeled pumps one afternoon as this threesome of Chinese women passed us, with two of them literally holding up the woman in the middle. I looked down and saw that she had bound feet. I'd never seen such a thing up close, of course. And these women then spoke to us. "They want to know how old you are," our translator explained. These ladies looked quite old, but perhaps they were actually my age. Anyway, I'd obviously made an impression on them in my relative youth and high-heeled feet.

Soon enough we were on China's North Vietnamese border, ensconced in a little hotel in a village where we picked lychee nuts off the overhanging trees as we walked down the street, trailed by packs of adorable local kids. Every day we planned to get a plane early in the morning to fly into North Vietnam, and every day we got up at six, packed our things, went to the airport and were told, "Sorry, the plane can't take off today, go back."

"Why?" we kept asking, "why can't the plane take off?"

We didn't know what to do with ourselves. We actually played bridge every night in four languages—me, Mary, and four men playing cards in that crazy hotel on the edge of China, two Russian guys, a Yugoslavian, and some other nationality that I now forget. "Just throw down your cards!" we'd holler. Nobody knew what anyone else was saying.

Finally, one morning we got up as usual, headed to the airport, and, amazingly enough, they let us on the plane, and off we went to North Vietnam. We passed over the 65th parallel north, a place I'd read about—it had been officially stated back home that we'd never bombed the 65th parallel north. I looked down, honey, and I saw bomb craters. Not that I was remotely familiar with bomb craters, but I'd never seen such holes before in my life. Those were bomb craters. Our plane, I realized, had been held up because of the bombing going on—bombing that our leaders were not even admitting to.

We landed in Hanoi. And there to meet us were twelve or fifteen little Vietnamese women, so lovely in their *bau dais*—these long gowns slit up the side—with flowers in their arms. Turns out they had been standing there with those flowers, awaiting our endlessly delayed arrival, for days. Still, it was one of the most beautiful moments I've had in my life. They embraced us and then we were put into a limousine with curtains on the windows. We were driven to the sort of town house you can find all over Washington, D.C. There, we were shown to lovely bedrooms, with canopied beds. Mary and I were absolutely exhausted. But first, they served us dinner in a beautiful dining room, with food that I will never forget—gourmet French-Vietnamese. The mind boggles. I still go to Vietnamese restaurants here in the city full of hope, but I'm afraid I will never again eat like I ate that first night in Vietnam.

It was *very* hot. And I was still wearing winter clothes. After we were in bed, a knock came at our door and a woman entered, saying, "Come. We have a tailor here. We want to fit you for some lighter clothing." A tailor appeared and measured us; he made me a whole dress in a single day, a sweet little green and white silk dress, and a couple of other light things, including my own *bau dai*. I still have the clothes today. Then they gave me ten yards of white silk to take home, which I also still have in my closet, pure silk-worm silk.

The meetings commenced the following morning. The women brought us torture victims—you know, to show what the Americans had done. They brought us maimed bombing victims: no arms, no legs, and faces scarred. Then we were taken down into a bomb shelter; they had bomb shelters dug all over the city—you picked up a manhole cover anywhere and there were stairs leading down. Finally, we were shown the remains of some American planes that had been shot down

I'd never seen war up close. The memory of it still haunts me.

What could we tell them? That we would get America to stop this war? No. The best we could offer was our word that some American women felt as they did, that this war was wrong. And that we hoped, by making contact, that we were connecting them somehow to women in America who felt as they did, women who did not view North Vietnam as our enemy.

We decided that we would now organize a follow-up meeting to our historic secret encounter. In Indonesia. We wanted a neutral place where we would bring more American women together with more Vietnamese women, a major meeting in Southeast Asia for all the forces who were against the war.

Mission more or less accomplished, Mary and I then made our way back through China to Moscow, and from there, home.

The ladies of North Vietnam with yours truly in one of my new silk dresses.

I'd never told Max and the girls about my North Vietnam plans. I couldn't tell anyone where I was going. It was illegal to be in North Vietnam. I would have had my passport taken away; I might have even gone to jail. I was no Jane Fonda. They would have just locked me up without fanfare. Hey, I worry about it today still. I know how vengeful this government can be. Look, we're in another Vietnam War right now in Iraq. Not that every war is wrong. But most are, and Vietnam was more wrong than most.

Just before leaving the Soviet Union for Vietnam, I'd written out all these postcards to my husband and family and given them to a friend with instructions to mail one off every other day. Now, of course, Max and the kids were at the airport to meet me in New York, and they were angry, *very* angry. Max, especially, was seething: "How could you? Where were you?"

"Wait a minute," I said, "you got postcards." I couldn't just tell him in the cab where I'd been, my lips were sealed. I didn't say anything until we were home and I could talk in the privacy of our bedroom.

None of my subsequent explanations got very far with Max. He was simply furious that I'd left him with two kids for so long, that he'd been forced to go off to work every night with the kids crying, "Mommy, Mommy, where's Mommy?"

This is why I ultimately chose not to go to Indonesia. Mary went. She met with the whole group. Not me. I refused to leave my family again. I decided that I had done my thing. I had to stay home. I had to take care of my girls.

For a long time, Rebecca and Deborah didn't know where I had been. My little excursion was executed entirely undercover.

Now I just faded back into motherhood. Though I never actually left the peace movement, per se, I did leave the activism, and it was a hard blow for me. My fundamental viewpoint, however, never changed. Not at all. I had involved myself in the movement as a moral issue, quite honestly. I was a dreamer. In fact, as I realize now, I was rather naïve.

Eventually Women Strike for Peace came to an end. And new causes and movements rose up. Yes, Women Strike for Peace finally died. But it was beautiful while it lasted.

CHAPTER 11

A PAYING JOB

IT WAS TELEVISION THAT KILLED THE BLUE ANGEL. All those acts, the great performers, were taken up by television and that was the demise of every fashionable nightclub on the East Side. People could sit home now and just watch. And so the scene changed, as it often does.

I'd stupidly encouraged Max to buy out his partner Herbert Jacoby, the Frenchman, the Prince of Darkness, back in 1962. I was not a businesswoman then. Jacoby wanted out. Luckily Max always had his little club downtown, so when everything was gone, when the Blue Angel finally went belly up, Max was left with his firstborn baby, the Village Vanguard.

As things deteriorated, I had to reconcentrate on the financial part of our life. I'd had carte blanche, you see, to do anything with my time—spend it on the telephone organizing Women Strike for Peace, doing public relations, and holding meetings in my home. Max never interfered; he was

165

most generous and kind. But now I had to work, not from my home but *for* my home and for my family, instead of for the peace movement. Ultimately, we would have to move from our luxurious apartment. We would have to give up the car and the housekeeper. And so I got a job—a *paying* job.

What did I do?

I went to work for a fashion designer whose clothes I'd once bought as a customer.

What did I do for her? I suffered. When she gave a fashion show at her little salon, I moderated it, "Beautiful gown, blah blah blah. It's made of *peau du soie*, blah blah blah; five thousand dollars." Her customers came in for fittings—everything was custom-made. When she did fittings, she'd say to me, "Hand me the pins," which I wanted to stick...!

I was eating humble pie, that's what I was doing. Max was financially at a low point. and I had to earn some money.

How did I meet the designer? That's a very good question. I don't remember. I know I gave her an apartment that I wanted, but Max didn't: two floors, a brownstone duplex on East 55th Street that Max didn't wish to live in because our ice cream friends, the Fields, had lived there first. Max was a very complicated man. I wanted those two floors with the garden, but Max said no. So I told my fashion lady about the place.

She was a very interesting-looking woman, I must say. She had no face, but when she painted it on, it was quite extraordinary. She also designed some wonderful clothes. She had an interesting body—rounded, like an odalisque—and she draped it well.

One evening Max and I went to the Royal Ballet, opening night at the Metropolitan Opera House. I borrowed a marvelous gown from my employer for the occasion. Max and I arrived a little bit late, and as we were rushing up the stairs, someone snapped my picture. The next day, there I was in the *New York Times*: "Mrs. Max Gordon—White Is In." It was the biggest photo on the fashion page. No one was more stunned than I. The *Times* had called and asked, "What's your name, and what's the designer's name?" So she was credited too. Prominently.

Of course, she called me up, so thrilled to have her name in print. "And when are you bringing the dress back?" she asked. "Soon," I said. And, like a fool, I did.

Shortly after that, I quit.

There was a woman in my building who lived with her daughter on the second floor. Very chic, spoke French without an accent. She had spotted my picture in the *Times* and, well, Madame from downstairs assailed me, shall I say. Very impressed with me, she was. Madame didn't know, of course, that my husband was having money problems, that I actually *worked* for the designer of the gown I'd been photographed wearing.

Evelyn and I became friends, of a sort. She was chasing after a gentleman who lived across the street—a stockbroker named Leo Farland who, as it turned out, liked art. Somehow this stockbroker got the rights to reproduce a poster of the Chagall tapestries that hung in the windows of the new Metropolitan Opera House at Lincoln Center. But he and she needed help—she was involved with him by now. The two of them were working out of his apartment in a co-op across the street on East 79th Street. But it was illegal. You

"The Dress" and me, as we appeared in the *New York Times*.

could not have a business in a co-op—they had to find some alternate location. So I helped them. And that spelled the beginning of my new life with the Farlands and what would become Poster Originals Ltd.

We located a little place on East 78th Street, a commercial space on the ground floor of a small building between Fifth and Madison, a block of handsome town houses and mansions. Then I asked Charles Gwathmey to design the store.

Max was very good friends with Robert and Rosalie Gwathmey, who had a son, Charles. Robert was a brilliant artist. Rosalie was a renowned fabric designer. Charles was, at that time, a young architect. I'd known Charlie since he was a little boy. The Gwathmeys lived right on Washington Square Park. Max and I used to have dinner with them at their home, and often young Charlie was present, though he later told me that I'd always terrified him.

What Charlie ultimately did for Poster Originals was very elegant. You entered down a little ramp into a long gallery space. On either side, slanting off the walls, were wide ledges, where we laid out the framed posters to be viewed. Up front, Charlie designed a huge book of plastic sleeves into which I inserted all the posters alphabetically (big job). Then toward the back was a curved wall where we sat behind a slit-like opening as if we were in a speakeasy. Back of that was a little kitchen.

For the next fifteen years, I slaved for Poster Originals. I devoted my life to that place. Max and I needed the money, and besides, I liked what I was doing. I didn't dislike it. I loved art, and still do. I was very involved, and I learned a lot too.

We only sold fine-art posters—excellent posters from the

Louvre and the like, from many top galleries too. This had never really been done before, apparently. People came from all over to buy those posters. Poster Originals was an innovation, and the owners (yes, eventually they married) became pioneers, though everyone thought that I owned the gallery because those two were mostly absent. Many people thought Poster Originals was mine.

I was always there, the front woman, at first alone. Eventually I hired other women to work with me. Fortunately I lived on East 79th so I could hop to work easily, open and close and things like that. Then we expanded to Madison Avenue. Almost simultaneously I opened another place for them down on Spring Street in SoHo. I knew someone who had a wonderful little shop there selling African art, very authentic things; she was a collector. Unfortunately the lady was closing up shop. We took her space. We took another space on Hudson Street for warehousing and framing the posters. Then we moved to an even bigger space, on West Broadway.

Oh, my goodness, yes, we were very successful for a while. Poster Originals was big.

The Blue Angel, meanwhile, finally went under completely in 1964. It hurt tremendously to lose it. Next we were forced to sell our house on Fire Island. I swallowed my love for that house, as well as my pride.

Still, I could not give up summers with my children. I tried Provincetown. Shoved the kids into a car—a borrowed car (we had to sell our own)—and took this rental apartment that Eugene O'Neill had once lived in, or so I was told. The rafters were painted with his writing; O'Neill had written on the rafters. Not that it mattered to me.

A butterfly in the hand. Fire Island. Farewell.

There was a creek in back, a little, smelly creek. The ocean was a car ride away. I'd look out at that little nothing piece of water, and I grew to hate that place so drastically I couldn't stand it any more. My kids didn't have friends, the cat was always getting lost, and the dog was crying. I piled everybody back into the car and said, "We're getting out of here."

Ultimately we all wound up in the Hamptons. Why the Hamptons? Why not? I was introduced to the Hamptons by Charlie Gwathmey. Charlie had come to see me just as we were selling our house on Fire Island. "Listen," he'd said, "I want to build a house for you over in the next community, a *round* house."

I said, "Charlie, I'm just *selling* my house, for the cash; you came at the wrong time."

So Charlie went to the Hamptons and built his round house for his mother in Amagansett. The night her house was finished, the Gwathmeys all came to the Vanguard to celebrate. "Come on," they'd said to me at the end of the night. "We'll drive you out to the Hamptons and show it to you."

"Wow," I said. "Okay. Max, can I go?"

It was dark, of course, when we arrived. I didn't know what the heck I was looking at. They placed me in the bottom bunk of a bunk bed in a little room—not a crummy-looking bunk bed, a pretty elegant little bunk bed, but still. In the morning, I woke up and the sun was shining in the windows. I looked out and fell in love immediately with what today is, I suppose, the most famous house in the Hamptons, from an architectural point of view, the Gwathmey house.

Obviously I couldn't have the Gwathmey house. But I did begin renting a house across the street shortly thereafter. And just like that, I became a Hamptons person. I wound up spending ten summers out there.

In time, I got bored. On Main Street one afternoon I noticed that a little flower store had gone out of business. I called the owner of Poster Originals, who had a house in Bridgehampton, and said to him, "Listen, I saw some great space for us today in East Hampton."

"Take it," he said. And I did.

Evelyn, his wife, was on her vacation in Europe. When she came back and heard about this, she was rather furious.

I can be so unrealistic at times. I worked for those people as if their place was *my* place. What the hell was I thinking?

The East Hampton store became very successful too. Even in the Hamptons, I was now a working woman, far past the point of being just a beach person with my kids, or with Max, when he came out to visit.

As ever, Max would visit. I was something of a loner for parts of my marriage. Max had his work in New York. For us, there was constant, constant action—a lot of it gratifying, a lot of it very sad. Even when the summers ended and I returned to the city, I could still find myself quite alone. Of course, there was much that Max and I shared. When Max lost the Blue Angel, that was very sad. When we lost our 79th Street apartment, that was sad; our building went co-op and we couldn't afford it. Though something good came of even this. Friends told us about a wonderful place in the Village, on MacDougal Street, right where it hits Prince. A duplex, redone by an artist. He and his wife had the downstairs, and the two upper stories became ours. The artist had done an incredible job—stone floors, mahogany cabinets, the works. I was used to the Upper East Side, but I adjusted. Max loved the Village; he was happy to be back. And the Vanguard was now all that we had.

I had many friends from the peace movement who lived in Westchester. These women and I maintained very strong friendships. When they had a party, they always invited me and I always managed to get there. Alone. I couldn't attend with Max—he was working all the time. If he couldn't make it, did that mean I couldn't? And Max encouraged me to go.

I always needed a ride back to the city. And there were always offers, often from men. Some of them I accepted.

Afterward I'd say, don't call me. But some did.

There are people in and out of everyone's life. The point is, these men were, in a sense, the glue in my marriage. Certain people help you keep your marriage together, when there's a missing component somewhere. It was fine, until it was over with them. Then it was over.

I look back on it now and think, Wow, did I do all that?

I did.

Preceding page: Jabbo Smith.

CHAPTER 12

JABBO

I WAS SITTING AT HOME reading the *Times* one Sunday morning in 1980. I always go to the arts section first—the heck with the news. And there I saw an ad announcing a new show at the Village Gate called *One Mo' Time*, featuring—the ad said—"Jabbo Smith on trumpet."

What?!

Jabbo Smith had died years ago, so far as I knew. I called my brother up immediately—he lived nearby. I said, "Philip! Jabbo Smith is alive and playing at the Village Gate!" We rushed over that very afternoon.

It was a terrific show. Vernel Bagneris had written *One Mo' Time*, all about a black theater troupe in the Deep South during the 1920s and how they had endured. There was a band, of course, onstage. And Jabbo Smith was the trumpet player! He sat up there in the left corner and he blew his head off! I tell you, we screamed with joy. I mean, he played with such strength for a man who was supposed to be dead.

The person who'd actually located Jabbo was the piano player in the band, Orange Kellin, a Swedish musician who'd been living in New Orleans. Somehow Orange Kellin had heard that Jabbo Smith was alive and well and living in Milwaukee. And Orange went looking for him.

He found Jabbo working at Avis Rent-a-Car. No one in Milwaukee had any idea who Jabbo Smith was. As Jabbo said, he had long since put his trumpet "under the bed."

He was still a very handsome man, with a stark, strong Southern face. After the show was over, Philip and I decided that we had to go backstage and talk to him. Of course they wouldn't let us in, but we waited and, finally, there came Jabbo shuffling out, looking at us very suspiciously. We were practically speechless, gazing upon our idol. Incredible!

He had a break before the evening show. "You know I live right near here," I said to him. "Maybe you'd like to come over and have some dinner." Very reluctantly, very dubiously, he agreed to come. We walked—it wasn't far. I offered him a drink, a brandy or something—which, knowing his habits now, I realize I shouldn't have. And we had some dinner, with Phil and his wife, Gertrude.

I just sat staring at this apparition. Philip and I reminded Jabbo how we'd known him back in Newark, New Jersey, at the Alcazar when we were kids. Then we walked him back to the Gate and sat through another show. I returned, thereafter, virtually every night.

In time, I got quite friendly with Vernel Bagneris, the creator of *One Mo' Time*, who was also in the show. The producers had found Jabbo an apartment on Fifth Avenue and Ninth Street. We now helped him furnish it. And gradually I got to know Jabbo too. He came over for more dinners. Suspicious man that he was, he nevertheless stopped holding me quite at arm's length. The show had by now become a big hit. And Jabbo was proving, shall we say, difficult. One day Vernel asked me if I would consider becoming Jabbo's manager—to see that he got to the show on time; you know, do the dirty work. I said okay, that I would certainly help, though I didn't really want any professional status in this. So I helped. I continued to help Jabbo until he died more than ten years later. I wound up accompanying him all over the world. Essentially I became his mother. That's what Jabbo needed, and I filled the bill.

He actually became something of a celebrity. Jabbo really was the star of *One Mo' Time*, and there was great curiosity about him both here and especially in Europe. Hundred of articles were written about him. Soon he was going on the road—Washington, D.C., Cleveland, Los Angeles, San Francisco. Often I would take Jabbo, drop him, and then come home. *His* expenses were paid for. *I* paid for myself. I was not a manager in any financial sense. But I did manage his money. I socked it all away in a bank. I got him into BMI so he could finally collect royalties on music he'd written. Jabbo still had a house in Milwaukee—I tried to sell it for him. He had family land in Georgia. I went to the depths of Georgia to look at this land that had been left to him by his grandfather. Gorgeous, tall, timbered land with fantastic pine trees. I wanted to sell it all and give him the money so he could be a self-sufficient old man and not have to do what old people without money have to do.

He wouldn't sell it. I had a buyer—the local tax collector, actually. Jabbo said he wanted to keep the land and plant soybeans on it. Yeah, right. In the end, I wound up giving this land away to one of his long-lost cousins in Philadelphia after Jabbo died, a cousin who'd never cared about Jabbo, who'd never even come to see him. Jabbo also had a sister in Philadelphia whom he was fond of: Ethel. She died. Jabbo didn't go to her funeral—*I* went to her funeral. "She's not going to know whether I'm there or not," Jabbo said, "you go." I must have been nuts.

This was a very strange period in my life. Insofar as Jabbo Smith was concerned, I took over. I put myself in charge of things. And it felt good.

Jabbo played the New York jazz club circuit and the Kool Jazz Festival. He went back to Chicago for a reunion with Ikey Robinson, the great banjo player he'd recorded with in the 1920s. Eventually calls came from Europe—not for *One Mo' Time*, but for Jabbo himself, from record collectors who still idolized him. They were doctors and lawyers, non-professional musicians who had their own small bands. They brought Jabbo over to play with them, in France, Switzerland, Italy, and Holland.

In March 1982, Jabbo played Rodez, Montpellier, Nîmes, Limoges, Albi, Nice, and Toulon in France; Geneva, Switzerland; and Turin, Italy. I took care of that trip, and, hey, I also went. We were driven around France in a beautiful BMW belonging to a great admirer of Jabbo's, Dr. Michel Bastide, an ophthalmologist–trumpet player with a band called the Hot Antique who'd first invited us to Europe. Jabbo and I sat in the back of Michel's BMW the whole way. If you want to see France, that is the way to see it.

There were other trips to Europe, including one to the Netherlands I will never forget. I correspond with those people to this day—"the Hot Dogs," they called themselves—especially Marc Van Nus, the trumpet-playing bandleader who so loved Jabbo. Sweetest people in the world. And such jazz fans.

I even went with Jabbo to Germany once, in 1986. Don Cherry took us—the avant-garde pocket trumpeter and Ornette Coleman's partner in crime. That was one of the weirdest combinations I could imagine: Don Cherry and Jabbo Smith.

I'd gotten Jabbo a couple of gigs at the Vanguard; I'd made Max book him. Well, one night Don Cherry was playing there with his group. Now, you can't get more far out than Don Cherry; he was wonderful. I introduced Don to Jabbo, and Don just fell in love, so much so that he hired

With Jabbo at the Vanguard, May 1987.

Jabbo to play in his band. Jabbo couldn't blow the trumpet very well anymore, but he still played a mean valve trombone. Jabbo and Don also scatted together on "Sweet Georgia Brown." Amazing. This big German promoter heard them at the Vanguard and booked them for a tour. I was included in the invitation because no one could get Jabbo on a plane. I was like an appendage.

Arriving in Berlin, we were put into a very nice little hotel on a quiet street, where I immediately got the willies. Kept hearing jackbooted footsteps. *Brr!*

The auditorium turned out to be almost as big as Madison Square Garden, in the round and just huge. The rest of the performers were all very modern jazz groups from everywhere; this was not your Dixieland crew. The place was packed. I stood in the wings. One band after another came out—each one more dissonant and esoteric. Then Don did his thing before finally introducing Jabbo, who entered. He now had a cane. He came out slowly, this tall, still-handsome old man in a wonderful suit—I now had suits made to order for him. He moved to the microphone in front of that huge house and softly started to sing the song "Love." I tell you, the audience went crazy. I'd never heard anything like it in my life. He got to their hearts. What an ovation! After listening to all that "art," this crowd of Germans finally heard true "soul." I stood back there with my wonderful new tape recorder and forgot to push the *on* button. I got back to the hotel, pushed *play*, and *nicht*! I was heartsick.

It seems to me now that everything I've done in my life prepared me for taking over the Village Vanguard. From the very first jazz record I bought as a kid, one experience after

Jabbo and his horns onstage.

another brought me closer, without my knowing it, to that ultimate destination. Managing Jabbo Smith's life was certainly no exception. All that looking after Jabbo brought me back into the jazz world, from a business sense. I realize this now.

Jabbo's first stroke came in 1989. I attended to him thereafter with great care. Placed him in a nursing home here in the Village—a terrible nursing home that I went to and visited virtually every day, fighting with everyone there to get him better care, schlepping Jabbo up to the roof in his wheelchair to get some fresh air. Things finally got so bad that he had to go into St. Vincent's Hospital. The call came early one morning in January 1991 that he had died. I went to his bedside and held his hand. And I cried. He was eighty-one.

CHAPTER 13

THE END OF A GORDON AGE

T<small>HERE WAS A MAN FROM</small> E<small>NGLAND</small> who had come into Poster Originals very often when I worked there, a very gifted man—he was an art director and a book designer, very artistic. Brian Rushton was his name. He and I had become friends. Brian loved jazz. I'd escort him down to the Vanguard sometimes.

Brian was working at the Brooklyn Museum as head of the merchandising department—the Gallery Shop, where they had begun to sell reproductions of objects in the museum collection, a very pioneering concept. At some point, Brian needed help and asked me if I would be interested in coming to work there. I was not working at the time. Actually, I was trying to think what I could do—me, with no college education. I had no particular talents. Still, Brian hired me. Suddenly I was the merchandising manager at the Brooklyn Museum. I'd never done anything like it before in my life. But that was okay. I liked jewelry and beautiful bibelots with historic content.

I began driving out to Brooklyn five days a week; I had a little secondhand car that Jabbo had given me. Then Brian tacked on another title, that of "head book buyer," which I liked best. I sat at my desk at the museum and all these publishers' salesmen came to see me with their big catalogs and I'd weed through their lists. I loved that. I'll never forget one in particular. I turned a page in this catalog and there was the title: *Jelly Roll, Jabbo and Fats,* by the great jazz writer Whitney Balliett. I let out such a shriek. Jabbo! I hadn't known about this! I immediately ordered a dozen copies—not for the museum but for me.

I was working at the Brooklyn Museum when Max really began to slow down. That's when he began talking to people about selling the Vanguard, or rather *they* began talking to *him*. Who were "they"? The Japanese. And Max's so-called friends. All of them hanging around, hovering, wondering what was going to happen next.

Max was now not feeling well at all. He would call me at the museum late in the afternoon, saying, "I'm not doing so good today"—and I'd go directly to the Vanguard after work and start opening up for him. Just a little daily thing. I'd sit in the kitchen of the club and phone Max back to say, "I did this and now I'm going to do that." I figured things out. It's not that difficult. I mean, I do have a brain.

Still, Max never asked me to take over. He just kept on courting potential buyers for the club—or rather allowed himself to keep on being courted. And I said nothing. I was not going to interfere.

Except once. The Japanese finally put a deal on the table,

With Max and President Jimmy Carter at a White House jazz party, June 1978.

and they weren't offering enough. I couldn't help myself. I said, "Max! Hey! This is a big bunch of nothing." And he listened. Otherwise, I went along with him totally—his willful *in*ability to know what to do.

Max Gordon simply never dreamed of me, Lorraine Gordon, his wife, taking over his club, the Village Vanguard. I know that. He didn't think. . . . I don't know what he thought. . . . That I wasn't capable? That I was a woman?

Very old-fashioned man. I was a wife to him. I'd raised the children. I worked on the side. He didn't think very much about what I could do or could not do. Never thought about it.

One day I actually helped him open the door of the Vanguard. His hands were getting a little feeble. There was a gate and two locks, and I said, "Here, give me the key, let me do that."

He said, "No, you don't know how to do this."

And I said, "What do you mean I don't know how to do it? You don't have to be a brain surgeon to open a door!" But that's the way he was with me. "Go look pretty, go buy something, go take care of the kids, go work."

The only husband I ever got involved with, business-wise, had been Alfred Lion, with whom I truly did work, night and day. But when I married Max—ha!—I became a lady of leisure. I mean, I worked—on the outside, in other jobs. And the peace movement, that was work, I mean full-time. I always worked, one way or another. But at the Blue Angel? Oh no. And I never interfered in the Vanguard at all. Except to discuss music with Max. Yes, that's the one thing I knew as much about as Max did. Maybe more.

He was a terrible sleeper. He'd sleep in snatches—innings, he called them: first inning—up, that's all, can't sleep anymore. Second inning—a little more sleep. He was just not a healthy man. He'd lived a hard life; those hours are not easy. And he always had that cigar in his mouth.

I just didn't think he would die. Ever. I thought Max was eternal, that he'd go on, complaining all the while. But then he got worse. And finally I gave up my job at the museum, it had gotten to be too much going back and forth.

194

He went into the hospital. This was in April 1989. I thought he was going in for one of his routine problems. He'd had a lot of them, mostly with his throat—we were forever taking Max to St. Vincent's emergency room. Everybody knew him there; the interns would say, "Oh, yeah, Max from the Vanguard." But this time something different seemed to be happening. And I couldn't find his doctor. I called him—my daughters and I were in the emergency room—and left a desperate message: "Max is back in the emergency and I don't like the way it looks." I never heard back from that doctor. And now they had Max up in the intensive care unit with a million machines hooked up to him. "What is all this?" I asked. "This is not what we brought him in for."

A doctor came to me then, a doctor I didn't know, who said to me, "You have to make a decision—to operate or not. Because whatever this is, it's got to be looked into. Now."

I didn't know what to say. My two daughters, Rebecca and Deborah, were with me, and now the three of us sat there trying to make a decision. Finally, I said, after consulting with them: "Yes, operate." What did I know? I was worried sick.

Well, he never came out of that operation. And Deborah, Rebecca, and I—all crumpled up and crying—eventually we walked across the street, across Seventh Avenue, like we had a million times before, to the Vanguard. And I closed it. For that night. Just put up a sign: "Closed for the night." And the next day I was there working, and it was open. And from that day on, I've been there. In charge. Totally.

Of course, I had to deal with Max's funeral. We had it at St. Peter's, the jazz church, on East 54th Street, just a block or so from where the Blue Angel had been. St. Peter's was so packed, I couldn't believe it. That Max had made so many friends in his lifetime, it was remarkable.

And then I began, well . . . running the Village Vanguard. Booking. Everything. Did I ever consider selling it? No, never. What for? I never said a word to any of the people who'd been hovering. I let them play their games; I watched them. But nobody had consulted with me in any way whatsoever. And I didn't consult with anyone now.

Still, I knew what was on certain people's minds. I mean, everybody wanted a piece of the action. What do you think they're talking about today: What's gonna happen when Lorraine goes? And I say, hey, you got any ideas?

I really had wonderful help right off. My daughter Deborah came in to work with me. I also got rid of some people who'd been taking advantage of Max. You see, Max did everything himself. He didn't need any help. I needed a little help. I wasn't going to be a martyr. There was a lot of work there. It was easier for Max. When he first started out, the Vanguard was just a little poetry place, and Max gradually learned everything himself.

To this day, he doesn't know I'm running the club. He just didn't dream of it. And I think, Max, you'd be proud of me. If you only knew.

"God bless her for keeping that place alive. It holds the spirits. But the first time I played there, man, I was totally afraid of her."

—Roy Hargrove
Trumpeter

Preceding page: Bill Cosby's cigar, November 1990.

CHAPTER 14

THE MRS. TAKES CHARGE

MAX GORDON HAD GREAT TASTE and almost impeccable instincts. In 1957, he began reinventing the Village Vanguard as a jazz club exclusively, more out of necessity than anything else. Max was finding it increasingly difficult to book the comics and the nightclub performers who had carried the Vanguard. Television was consuming them all, as it would eventually consume the Blue Angel. So Max steered the Vanguard more and more toward jazz. Only in retrospect does this seem brilliant. But it was. It's a long way from the Weavers to Bill Evans, Miles Davis, Sonny Rollins, and John Coltrane. You think I understood what Coltrane was doing when I heard him at the Vanguard in the sixties? I should say not. I didn't know what the hell I was listening to. Max, however, was a man open to anything good when it came to music—to all kinds of art, in fact. Max loved the theater. He loved good movies. I remember once before we were married when I went to see *The Red Shoes* with him and arrived

201

late. Max gave me such a lecture. He didn't want to miss a minute of anything. Same with painting and fine art. Max fell in love very early on with Jacob Lawrence, whose work he bought, not knowing or caring how big Jacob Lawrence would become.

Max booked a lot of acts I couldn't or wouldn't today. John Cage appeared at the Vanguard in the late 1950s, as did Jack Kerouac. These were Sunday night things that were out of the ordinary. Poetry readings. I recall Langston Hughes at one.

The litany of jazz names Max brought in during this period established the Vanguard's peerless jazz identity for all time: Carmen McCrae; Charles Mingus; Thelonious Monk; Stan Getz; Ben Webster; Mose Allison; Anita O'Day; Teddy Wilson; Miles Davis; Horace Silver; Chris Connor; Dizzy Gillespie; George Shearing; Johnny Griffin; Lambert, Hendricks & Ross; Zoot Sims; Max Roach; Red Garland; Ahmad Jamal; Dinah Washington. Max booked Aretha Franklin as early as 1960; Ornette Coleman and Nina Simone on the same bill in 1961; Roy Eldridge and Lenny Bruce on the same bill, also in 1961, for over a month. Carol Sloane, who still appears at the Vanguard regularly, debuted in August 1961, opening for Oscar Peterson, then sang opposite Lenny Bruce for a month in 1962. Carol tells the story of Lenny asking her to go back into the little dressing room Max had then for the performers, just to the right of the stage, to get Lenny's socks. "I left my socks hanging there," he told her. So Carol went in and got Lenny's socks, thinking, "These socks of his are very heavy." Of course, they were filled with Lenny's stash of God knows what.

I remember the "Speak-Outs" Max hosted in the sixties on Monday nights, beginning in December 1964, open forums led by guest speakers like Leroi Jones, Allen Ginsberg, and Andy Warhol. We had a psychedelic one with Timothy Leary; we handed out jelly beans in lieu of LSD, and we had a lava lamp made for the occasion that sits on the bar to this day.

Mingus was practically the house band in 1965 with his Jazz Workshop Orchestra. Once, Coleman Hawkins played opposite him. I used to go into the kitchen and just stare at Hawkins; I was so in awe of this giant who'd recorded the definitive "Body and Soul" that I'd grown up listening to. I couldn't believe it was actually Coleman Hawkins sitting there with his horn, surrounded by our stacked crates of beer.

Sonny Rollins also played the Vanguard plenty in the sixties and seventies. You think I could get him back today? Never. Sonny wouldn't consider anything so lowly. I've stopped asking. Let him go play on a bridge.

Max was not a jazz aficionado. But he listened—both to the music and to the musicians. Miles Davis tipped Max off to many new talents; the keyboardist and singer Shirley Horn was one in particular who played the Vanguard because of Miles. Hey, Max didn't know who Thelonious Monk was until I walked in the door. But when enough musicians told Max to hire someone, he usually did.

Stepping in for Max at the Vanguard was an enormous leap for me, in one sense. In another sense, it was just a natural progression, the most natural progression, really. Like Max, I was a pretty good listener too. And I really was a jazz aficionado. I'd been anonymous for a long time as Mrs. Max

Gordon. But I'd spent my whole life learning how to run the Village Vanguard, without knowing it.

I certainly had no fear. I knew that I could walk in there and pick up that phone and call a musician or talk to an agent. I just got into the swim as fast as I could, just held my nose and jumped in.

I booked whom I liked: Joe Henderson, Charlie Haden, Donald Byrd, Winard Harper, Bill Frisell. Some bookings were great; some turned out not to be. Many of these musicians already had been playing for Max forever. A number of others I discontinued pretty quick. I could see we needed new blood around the place.

Business was not great when I took over. I was very worried about saving pennies. I looked closely at everything. What's this bill for? What's that bill for? Do I need this? Do I need that? I didn't need a linen service for $200 a week. There was a laundry right across the street for $1.98. I cut the linen service out. Max had a beer company that was outrageously overcharging him. I found someone who would supply the same beer for half the price.

It was all a matter of learning on the job. There were people who'd been working at the Vanguard a long time, and most were in some ways helpful. The waitresses knew how to do this; the bartender knew how to do that. Max had a terrible accountant whom I finally got rid of. Max had a wonderful landlord whom I still treasure.

It took me a while, but I figured things out. I began to ask questions right out loud, "How come there were so many people in the club tonight and there's so little money to show for it? There were over a hundred people here, so where's the bread?"

In the Vanguard kitchen with Deborah and Rebecca celebrating my birthday, October 1989.

Elementary, Dr. Watson.

And soon a few more long-time employees were receiving their walking papers from Mrs. Gordon.

First and foremost, the musicians had to be paid. I liked to pay the musicians on time, every night. I still prefer it that way, and so do the musicians.

Money was short my first year in charge. We remained entirely dependent, of course, on how many people walked through the door, plus whatever drinks we sold. I now charge twenty dollars for admission; it was fifteen dollars when I took over.

I had to find a bookkeeper I could put my faith in. Max's bookkeeper, as I said, was just not for me. In the end I found someone through my lawyers. I liked him; he liked me—he sent over a fellow who is still my bookkeeper today and very much responsible for helping me master the mechanics of the Vanguard's affairs, especially its relentless overseers:

the board of health, the fire department, the I.R.S.—all the departments that run your business in New York City, whether you like it or not.

My own business habits didn't hurt either. I pay every bill before it's due. I'm a stickler for that. I can't stand bills. I pay everything fast. As a result, I don't owe anyone a penny.

So when did things pick up? Gradually. The Village Vanguard had its own name and its own spirit of survival. I cannot take any credit for that. People kept coming through the door just to be at the Village Vanguard. Many of them didn't really care who was playing, and they certainly didn't care who was running things. But some were grateful, terribly so. "Thank you for keeping it open," they said to me. Such dear people, these Vanguard lovers. They gave me strength.

"She's one of the only club owners left that you deal with on a personal basis these days. Lorraine embraces the whole history of jazz. Yet she functions in the here and now. Just like us. Jazz musicians have to have the whole history of jazz at their fingertips, yet still be themselves in the music. It's the same."

—Joe Lovano
Saxophonist

CHAPTER 15

ALIVE AT THE VILLAGE VANGUARD

People who work nine to five know that they have to be up at seven. I did that scene. I woke up with the sun and went to work, came home, and made dinner for my children and my husband. Working those hours, I often was too tired to go out with my husband afterward. Max wanted me to go. But I couldn't. Today, however, my clock has been reset. I'm living on Max time. Like my mother used to say, you can get used to anything.

I open up the Vanguard front door at three P.M. almost every afternoon. The building itself, the whole structure, is two stories tall, with us in the basement. The Vanguard has a sewer running directly beneath it and all the problems inherent in occupying a basement. Every time it rains we run around with towels trying to cover the leaks. My landlord has caulked most of those, but he still calls whenever it rains to ask, "Is everything okay?"

The building has been around only seventy-five years.

That's not so very old. Back in 1921, after the city plowed a subway link through Greenwich Village that sliced many building lots into odd shapes, a developer named Morris Weinstein threw up our triangular building, renting space in it to, among others, a cleaners on street level and a speakeasy in the basement appropriately dubbed the Golden Triangle.

Until fairly recently, the first floor above us still had shops in it: there was a lovely little jewelry store and a nice little hairdresser to the left of my door and a men's clothing store to the right. The man who owned the clothing store lived on the building's top floor—his apartment ran the entire length of the building—and he managed to almost burn the entire building down one night by smoking in bed and igniting an enormous fire that the Vanguard only managed to survive because it was in the basement.

Just right of my front door today is what I originally believed to be just a nail-polishing place. Turns out it offers everything from a massage to a blow-dry. (I mean it, the words are literally plastered on the window.) Left of my door is a pizza parlor. Not that I don't like pizza, but everything about this parlor is so garish, tons of neon. I just try to squeeze into my doorway without looking left or right. It's a shame. A nice restaurant in the building would be wonderful.

On my way over from my apartment I usually stop at the post office for the bigger mail that I'm sent—the magazines and newspapers, the tapes, and CDs that the mailman can't fit through our mail slot. Max used to have a bright red folding gate guarding the front door. That's the gate I helped him open once. Suddenly, after Max was gone, I got a notice from the city announcing that our gate was illegal. Illegal!

That gate had been here longer than most people. I started to look around after receiving this notice. The city, you know, is just teeming with storefront gates of every variety. No matter. Down mine came. I still have it in the basement. In its stead I had new front doors put on, also bright red, with fancy locks made in Israel, of all places. They cost a lot of shekels.

So there I am virtually any afternoon, just a lady and her two six-hundred-dollar locks. (When the weather gets cold, the top one freezes and I have to call the pizza guy next door to help me open it.)

Then, down the stairs I go. At the bottom of the stairs I unlock another door, which leaves me where?

Alone, in a big, dark room.

I fumble my way around the nearest wall. A few times I've bumped right into the wall. Being left-handed, with no sense of direction whatsoever, I at least know that when I go crash, *bang*, I'm in the wrong wall. Eventually, I locate the kitchen lights and switch some on. But not all of them. Lights, after all, cost money.

First thing that greets me in the kitchen is the answering machine, blinking and blinking away, because people have been calling for reservations since the night before. Soon the deliveries arrive: the beer, the wine. Musicians come by to rehearse; if it's Tuesday and they're opening that night, there's an afternoon sound check. And the phone, the phone, the phone keeps on ringing. While I'm there, I take many reservations down myself with a pen on a yellow legal pad.

Finally, around six P.M., I go home or out for dinner. I had a restaurant for years called Anton's around the corner from the Vanguard on West 4th and Perry Street. It was a real Village place, simple and nice—two waitresses, no glitz, just good food. Anton was the cook. He also was a musician—from the Pyrenees or Yugoslavia or something, I'm not quite sure. Anton cooked the way I like to cook at home myself. I dined at his restaurant two or three times a week. I brought all my musicians there and all my friends. I sent customers there too, those who asked for a restaurant recommendation. Everybody was happy with Anton.

Well, Anton is gone. His landlord decided, of course, that Anton wasn't paying enough rent. I was thunderstruck. It was like losing a lover.

Now my favorite dining establishment is my home. Always has been, really. When I'm home and have time to think about what I'm going to do in the kitchen, along with the fixings that I need, I can really cook. And I'm so relaxed when I cook. It's my therapy. I listen to music, often classical. Then it's back to the club before nine.

I have to get dressed, ditch the rags I wear during the day, put on makeup, and get a little more put together. Before too long I'm at my little table once again—first table on your left as you come in the door—talking to people, greeting musicians, listening to the music, and pointing wayward patrons toward the restrooms. Life begins all over. It's wonderful. I love it. Some nights the music is so fine I nearly burst. I want to poke someone and say, "Did you hear that?" Actually, I often do.

When I went to the Vanguard with Max Gordon, I never sat where I sit now. In fact, there was never even a table where I sit now. When I first started running things, I decided we needed a little more space down front, so we moved this two-seater from near the bandstand—we moved it back up against the side wall, stage right, at a point where one long red banquette ends and the hall to our kitchen begins.

Once I sat myself down, I realized I could see the whole club from this spot and also be near the front door. Before that I'd been sitting at the bar, last seat against the rear wall, which also had given me a bird's-eye view of the club, *and* of the bartender. Max used to sit back there too, but not at the bar. Max sat at a table opposite the bar, where *he* could watch the bartender, and sleep better. Now, though, I can see everything and everyone and still slip back into the kitchen to transact a little quick business or even give up my table if we need it.

One night in particular, I remember sitting there just before the first set and noticing a man down front at a table near the piano, waiting for someone to join him. Suddenly I heard the name "Kissinger" behind me at the door. I looked up. And there he was. I mean, who could mistake that *punim*—that face?

I jumped up and cornered him, "Excuse me. That will be twenty dollars for admission plus ten dollars minimum for drinks, please. No credit cards. Cash or travelers checks only." Kissinger took out his wallet, paid up, and then put out his hand to shake mine. I pulled my hand back and walked away; I tried to make it as much of a snub as I possibly could. Obviously I couldn't deliver a speech, though I sure would have liked to. I would have liked to ask him, "How many boys did you kill in Vietnam?" It was all I could do to not let him touch me. Henry Kissinger! At the Vanguard! If I'd had any guts, I would have thrown him out.

Turned out that the man down front waiting for Kissinger was Václav Havel, at that time the president of Czechoslovakia.

It's funny. The Vanguard really is a leveler. It brings all kinds of people together in the name of one thing: great jazz. Even the loudest big shots get quiet at the Vanguard. They simply have to.

The room seats a hundred twenty-three people, legally, a hundred thirty with a little squeezing. It's quite a wonderful room. I always appreciate it anew after I've visited another club and then come home again to the Vanguard in all its warmth. It is an enveloping space—triangular in shape, like the building it sits beneath, cut like a piece of pie. The bandstand is at one end—the wider part—and the room then narrows as you move toward the back, near the bar.

The acoustics are exceptional. Some believe that the shape of the room largely makes this so. I couldn't say. All I know is, nowhere else does jazz music sound better.

There are many famously fine photographs hanging on the walls, but they weren't always there. The Vanguard used to have sublime murals by an artist named Paul Petroff, who is alive and well and living in the state of Washington. I still keep in touch with him. Paul painted his murals in the early 1940s. As a young kid going to the Vanguard, I fell in love with them. They were very sophisticated and charming, very witty. Over the years, they became an essential part of the Vanguard experience. But eventually Max took them down, for his own reasons. No, they were not painted over. If they had been, I would be scraping the paint off them right now. To me, Paul Petroff's murals were an expression of my love for jazz

Segments of Paul Petroff's long-lost Vanguard murals. The top one covered the balcony wall of the club; the one below ran along the bar wall.

music; they somehow summed it up for me (remember, I had wanted to be an artist in my youth). But Max tired of them.

Yet another set of murals went up and came down during my years as Mrs. Max Gordon. This set was actually painted by my brother, Philip, including a kind of Cubist image of a man and a woman that remains on the back wall to this day. Floods eventually brought down the rest of my brother's murals. That's when the photos went up. Max had a ton of photographs; practically every time a musician played the Vanguard he gave Max a head shot of himself for publicity purposes. Record companies also sent pictures. After Max nailed a few of these up on the walls, many photographers offered him more, great photographers like William P. Gottlieb, Roy DeCarava, and Carol Friedman. Who wouldn't want their work on the walls of the Village Vanguard? It's a free exhibition space. But those pictures were put up helter-skelter. When I took over, they had no pattern or arrangement, which really drove me crazy. I mean, I'd worked in a poster gallery for years, where I was responsible for hanging the art.

I finally took everything down—something I'd been aching to do—and redid the whole scheme. First, I put green felt up on the walls, the very darkest green I could find, darker than the darkest pool-table top. The color actually had been on the walls before, years earlier, and was still visible in places. I traveled all over this town, up and down, with a little sample chip in my hand before finally finding the felt that I wanted in a tiny shop on the Lower East Side. I hung that felt with the help of a person who worked for me; we stapled it ourselves. It remains a fine background for pictures.

I then rehung all the photographs. I didn't frame them, though. I shrink-wrapped them, heat-sealed—which is nice because you can just wipe them clean.

I also added some new photographs to the walls. My favorite? I do love the picture of Tommy Flanagan near the piano that Jack Vartoogian took. That one is especially beautiful.

Like most regulars, I too have all kinds of questions about the club's history. A few of these questions I even have answers to. For example: Did Duke Ellington ever play the Vanguard? Not to my knowledge. But he did sit there and listen sometimes as an audience member. Do I remember who it was that he came to see? No. But I sure remember on one occasion, sitting beside him. Such a thrill. What about Count Basie? Oh, yes! Max somehow hired Basie and his band for one night that I will never forget (except for the date, I'm afraid). No one knows about it today beyond the people who were there. I sat in the front row that night. The Vanguard practically levitated.

The levels in the club—the room has a kind of terraced balcony built into its tiny confines, and other oddities. Who built them? I don't really know. After the Golden Triangle speakeasy, a theater occupied this basement. And I do know that there are elements still extant today from that theater, including our ladies' and men's rooms. There are also some big lighting wheels that have survived. They're in our back hall—anyone can see them. The theater's stage, as I understand it, was in the back of the house, where our bar is. Maybe what we call our "balcony" today, was built by the theater people.

There also still is a dance floor in front of the stage, a little

wooden floor. I've never carpeted it, though there's no dancing anymore. When I first met Max we used to dance together
at the Vanguard all the time; there was dancing nightly to the
great Clarence Williams Trio. Max did the schottische and I
did the jitterbug. Some of those were very late nights.

Today I generally stick around for one show and a half on
any given evening. I mean, I get tired too. I'm usually home
by midnight, one at the latest, though sometimes I stay till
closing. Problem is, when I get home I start to read; I read in
bed and then I can't sleep. Reading is a very big part of my
life, and when do I have time to read otherwise? As a result
I don't always get enough sleep, and that's not terrific.

I make a lot of connections at night. That's one reason I
hang out so late—you never know who's going to walk
through that door. Not long ago we held a fortieth-
anniversary celebration for the Vanguard Big Band. Forty
years ago, a great trumpet player named Thad Jones and a
fine drummer named Mel Lewis asked Max if they could
bring a big band they'd been developing to play for one
night at the Vanguard, a Monday night. Max said yes. Max
liked what he heard. He invited them back the next Monday night, and the next. They became an institution. Thad
eventually died, then Mel. The Vanguard Big Band remains
a vibrantly alive sixteen-piece institution.

It's an incredible experience to hear them in their home
room. Usually that opportunity only presents itself on Monday nights. For the band's fortieth anniversary, I gave them
a week. One night, halfway through that week, the trombonist Slide Hampton showed up to sit in. I'd been trying to
book Slide Hampton for years. This time I cornered him,
and he said sure. That's how I get a lot of the musicians I

want. Maybe they won't ultimately appear. Maybe they will. If I see them and court them myself, I have a much better chance.

The good part about being the boss is, I don't *have* to stay till closing. I have a wonderful staff, and they close the place up. Jed Eisenman has been working at the Vanguard for at least twenty years. Jed started out working for Max. He loves jazz, lives for it, really. Jed left Bard College to hang around the Village Vanguard. Eventually I elevated his status and made him my right and left hand. Jed knows music. And he's often my memory. I'll say to him, "You know, the guy with the size-ten shoe?" and Jed will tell me who I'm thinking of. He's very sharp. I do what I want to, of course, and if Jed doesn't agree with me, that's tough, but it's wonderful to sound ideas off of him.

My crew is marvelous, if unorthodox. My daughter Deborah is my main player, along with Jed. The three of us run the club. Deborah was a filmmaker for a long time. When Max died, she knew her mother was working more or less alone. So she came in to help me. Deborah also has a phenomenal memory that I access endlessly. She and Jed have relieved me of all those nitty-gritty details I was so consumed with at the beginning. We're a real troika, working slightly different hours to cover the whole week.

Steven Kellam, whom you'll usually find at the door, makes our troika a quartet. Steve closes the club two nights a week and is invaluable in innumerable ways.

Everyone who works for me, I have found, possesses a second secret talent that the Vanguard somehow brings out of them. Steven Kellam also handles our Web site. He designed it. He also designed our caps. Caps, T-shirts, and baby socks—that's the extent of our souvenir industry at the Vanguard.

Alan at the door is a very quiet guy. Get one word out of him and you've done a lot. So quiet. Well, he also turned out to be a great soundman—*my* soundman. And he is so conscientious. He watches the room, if I'm not looking. Someone using a cell phone? Out. Taking pictures? Nope. Sorry. Taping the music? I don't think so.

How did they all get their start? Everyone starts in the kitchen. But the Vanguard doesn't serve food, you say; nothing's happening in the kitchen. That's what you think. The kitchen is actually the heart of the Vanguard. My office is there (or, I should say, my desk). The musicians are there, all congregating and hanging out. Plus, we have a dishwasher forever churning away. The beer has to be brought out. And the place has to be cleaned during the day. My club is clean as a whistle. Some *New Yorker* magazine writer not long ago described the Vanguard as "musty." Only in his mind, I want to tell you. I'd like to get my hands on that guy. There's no "musty" in my Vanguard. I'm a fanatic for cleaning.

The Village Vanguard hasn't served food for a long time. When did we stop? When the chef died. Elton was the chef. Elton died. Max said, "That's it. No more food."

It's must be over twenty years now. Elton made the best burgers and turkey sandwiches. Max had a big, old Vulcan stove in the kitchen, with the salamander symbol on top, a real classic. Elton would have a big tall pot going all the time with a turkey in it. The turkey would go in headfirst, and when one side was done, Elton would turn it over and cook the bottom; he had to do it in two stages because the pot was never quite big enough. Still, the taste was phenomenal. As were Elton's burgers. People would ask Elton how he got the burgers to come out so great, and he'd say, "Because Max buys the best meat there is.'"

The musicians always hung out in the kitchen at the Vanguard because they loved Elton's cooking (and because the club had no dressing rooms). That's how the kitchen tradition began. The guys hung out where the food was, while the dishes were being washed, while the phones were ringing. It became the place to be, and when Max stopped serving food, it just made the kitchen easier for the musicians to access. Nothing about that has changed to this day.

Charles Mingus, the brilliant, bear-like bass player and bandleader, would order-in meals when he was playing the Vanguard. I don't think anyone who didn't actually watch him eat can really understand the appetite Charles Mingus had. This one time I recall, Mingus's food arrived in a big package that he unwrapped in the kitchen. And it was raw meat. Which he ate, raw. This was not steak tartar. It was raw, ground meat, with nothing on it. Mingus was an enormous eater! He could not fill himself up. Did all that raw meat contribute at all to his final illness, Lou Gehrig's disease? Good question. It's very possible. The last time Max and I saw Mingus was at the White House, a big jazz party hosted by Jimmy Carter on the lawn. Charles was there in a wheelchair.

We also have the "Mingus Light" in the ceiling at the Vanguard. It's like a shrine; people come in asking to see it. It's a hole where Mingus took his bass and smashed a ceiling light one night. Max left the shattered enclosure of the light, and it became a landmark. On another occasion, Charles also ripped the upstairs front door off its hinges. I wasn't there that night; this is "as told" to me. Charles was furious with Max apparently because the sign out front had him billed as "*Charlie* Mingus." A lovely woman, a regular at the club, and a fine potter who happened to be a tiny person, actually lugged that door home. It was bigger than her. Who knows—she might still have it. But that was Mingus. Mingus was a terror.

I remember when Thelonious would play the Vanguard, his wife, Nellie, who was always watching Monk's health very carefully, would bring her blender with her and mix up health foods for him right there in the kitchen. She'd be on Thelonious's left, and on his right would be the Baroness Panonica de Koenigswater with her cigarette holder blowing cigarette smoke in his face. They were truly a ménage à trois. I always marveled at that.

When Monk was at the Vanguard, the baroness was present every night; she had her seat up on the "balcony." I'd known the baroness since I worked at Poster Originals on Madison Avenue; she would bring in art for me to frame, pieces she owned. I was known to her then as just Max Gordon's wife. I also saw her around Poster Originals' first gallery on East 78th. Across the street was one of the more notorious Dr. Feelgoods in town, famous for his so-called vitamin injections, most of which were just amphetamine, apparently. I spotted the baroness's Bentley often parked out front of that doctor's office. I'd watch Monk get out and go into this Dr. Feelgood, while the baroness came in to see me at Poster Originals. I didn't like that at all. I thought, What is Thelonious doing there? The doctor was subsequently tossed out; he lost his license.

She had a British accent and a Bentley and was a Rothschild. Charlie Parker literally had died on her sofa at the

Wynton, July 1991.

Stanhope Hotel, which, I suppose, remains her greatest claim to fame. She loved jazz and jazz musicians, and became known as something of a patroness. She certainly had her charm and was always lovely to me, but I was such a purist. The baroness loved Thelonious and the pianist Tommy Flanagan too. I thought Nellie was Monk's wife. But there was the baroness. Thelonious finally moved in with her—at another of her homes, across the river in Wee-hawken, New Jersey. It was in this house that Thelonious ultimately died. What more can I say?

Today the musicians come with their own women; they all seem to have their own Japanese sidekicks.

I kid a lot of the musicians. That's the way many jazz

musicians communicate, jokingly. I love to kid with them, especially in the kitchen when they're waiting to go on.

Wynton Marsalis in particular is a wonderful kidder. Wynton has never forsaken the Vanguard. He gets paid like everybody else; well, more or less—he has a manager who keeps bumping the number up a little, and I don't argue. Wynton deserves it. He's loyal. Whenever I need him, whenever I've asked him to be there, he's there. Whenever any of his men play the Vanguard, he usually shows up too.

I kid Wynton mostly about his clothes. He appeared recently in such an outfit! It was so beautiful—the tie, the shirt, everything. I walked up to him, got real close, and said, "You *look* expensive." And that horn of his, the one he's been playing lately—all gold and shaped like a rocket ship. I feel about it the way I felt about Dizzy's horn—with the bell pointing up to the ceiling, all bent out of shape. I kept looking up all the time when Dizzy played that thing to see where the notes were going.

How do I choose whom I hire? Basically I just start with what I know. I like what I like, so that's what I hire. I don't know anything else.

I also read everything about jazz that's available; I try to keep up with the jazz world—newspapers, magazines, books, and CDs. That's my life now. Honestly, I don't think of balance at all when I put together our booking schedule. Maybe I should, but I don't. I get who I want, when they're available. As a result, I sometimes have four straight weeks of trumpet players. But what's wrong with that?

Who were my proudest booking coups?

Chucho Valdés. And Martial Solal. Two brilliant non-American pianists: Chucho from Cuba, and Martial from

France (by way of Algeria). Chucho is the son of Bebo Valdés, the legendary music director of the famous Club Tropicana in Havana. Chucho also founded Irakere, probably Cuba's most successful contemporary jazz group; Irakere managed to score an American record contract and even a Grammy in the late 1970s. None of which I particularly cared about. I just knew that I loved Chucho's piano playing when I heard him in 1998, and had to have him at the Vanguard.

It took the trumpeter Roy Hargrove and his manager Larry Clothier, plus the wondrous Rene Lopez, an expert here in New York on Latin music and a great friend of Chucho's, to help me get my man. Rene brought me down to

With Chucho in Cuba. I won't say what year.

Cuba (yes, legally) and Rene introduced me to Chucho Valdés.

I was completely smitten. Oh, what a charming man! My first Cuban. So gentle. So amusing. So tall.

I now had to cut through disgraceful amounts of red tape. Under U.S. immigration law, the only appearances by Cuban musicians permitted in America had to be—by some bureaucratic definition—"cultural exchanges." Did an extended gig at a basement jazz club in Greenwich Village qualify as cultural exchange? On the morning of Chucho's scheduled opening in June 1999, his visa still had not been approved by the State Department. Yes, Chucho was on a plane to New York from Havana. The problem was getting him off that plane.

It was nearing nine P.M. when I got word that Chucho was being detained at Kennedy Airport. The house was already packed for his first set. Three hours later we were all still waiting. And then suddenly people were shouting in the stairwell, "He's here!" And there came massive, six-foot-eight-inch Chucho marching down the Vanguard stairs, his arms filled with flowers. Bouquets of them. The room went nuts. Chucho pushed his way to the piano, played three notes and announced so sweetly, "I am very tired. Please come back tomorrow."

Of course, he slayed everyone that week. A year later, I had him back; that run resulted in one of the best recordings ever made at our little club, *Chucho Valdés: Live at the Village Vanguard*. Thereafter, I also went back to Cuba a couple of more times to visit Chucho. We even fantasized about opening a club together in Havana.

I miss him. Now I can't go there; he can't come here! I am

so angry at my country. Chucho Valdés can travel anywhere in the world that he wants to, this dangerous man. Anywhere, that is, except to George Bush's America.

No one really remembered the name Martial Solal, when I got this bug in my head that I had to have him at the Vanguard. This was in 2001. Don't ask me why. I'd known about Martial Solal most of my life as a jazz record collector and listener. I knew that he'd played with Sidney Bechet in Paris. I knew his score for the Jean-Luc Godard film *Breathless*. I knew his brilliance both as a pianist and as a composer. But I'd certainly never met him. I had no personal contact.

Still, when I want someone, I usually find him . . . and get him. And somehow I found my way through to Martial Solal in Paris. He didn't speak English so well. Didn't I speak French? *Non.*

We did manage to discuss money. I had to. I knew that I wanted Martial Solal, but I wasn't at all sure anyone else did. How would he draw? Finally, I got Martial on a plane to New York.

Unfortunately it was the day before 9/11.

Tommy Flanagan was supposed to open at the Vanguard that night—which was a Tuesday—but of course he didn't. We were closed for three days before Tommy finished his foreshortened week. Then, Martial stepped up to play our Steinway grand.

And nobody came. Martial played magnificently, but he did virtually no business. Which was hardly his fault. The Vanguard suffered for months after 9/11. Everyone around here did. This neighborhood of ours was on the edge of a war zone.

Yet, we survived that too. The Village Vanguard outlasts even terrorists.

Speaking of terrorists, many musicians whom I don't know come up to me at the club and ask for gigs. They come with tapes and CDs, biographies, even managers sometimes. Telling them no is the hardest thing for me. I'm actually running out of excuses—they counter whatever I say. Finally, I just have to tell them, "Look, I'll hold on to this CD of yours, but it isn't likely that you'll be hearing from me." Sometimes I just say, "Look, I only book people who've played here before." Which is almost but not entirely true, of course.

"How do I get a start?" they ask me. Good question. Go to a smaller club. Start there. But you can't start here. This isn't a jumping-off place anymore. Maybe it was years ago, but not now. I have to fill this room every night to survive.

There's a pianist named Ethan Iverson who performed here as a sideman not long ago. I fell in love with his playing and booked him a few times more as a sideman. Finally, I said to Ethan, "How about your own group?" Boom. Done deal. Moreover, the band that he brought in for the occasion, the Bad Plus, has had a lot of success since. So it does happen, but very rarely, that someone actually gets their big break at the Vanguard today.

Recently the wonderful alto saxophonist Lou Donaldson was due to perform. For many years now, Lou has been playing here with the organist Dr. Lonnie Smith. Pre-Lonnie, Lou always had appeared with a quartet—sax, piano, bass, and drums—before announcing to me one day that the pianist for his next gig would be an organist named Lonnie Smith. Okay, I admit, I'd never heard of Lonnie Smith, but Lou wanted him, so we schlepped an organ down the stairs

Ethan Iverson (right) at the Vanguard on his first gig as a leader, along with his former boss, dancer-choreographer Mark Morris, for whom Ethan worked as musical director.

for this Lonnie Smith to play. It weighed a ton. And proved a huge hit, in the hands of Dr. Smith.

On this particular occasion, though, Lou informed me that Lonnie would not be able to make it. He had a previous engagement.

"Oh, what am I going to do?" I said to Lou, "I've got to have Lonnie."

"Relax," Lou said, "I'll get us another organ player."

"I don't want another organ player."

"All right," Lou says, "I've got this pianist from St. Louis."

"Is he bluesy?" I asked. "Is he strong?"

"You'll like him," Lou said.

"What's his name?"

"Ptah," says Lou. "P-T-A-H. Williams."

"What, did you forget a letter there?"

"No," Lou said, "that's his name."

I didn't want to disappoint Lou. He's a great musician. But I didn't want any of this Ptah. Still, I kept my mouth shut. "Just get a good bass player," I told Lou.

A few weeks later they opened. I tell you, this Ptah was a killer! What a piano player! He's in his forties. I don't know where he's been hiding. What energy! He just rocked the place. Broke a string on the piano. "The next one you pay for," I told him.

But finding a Ptah is precisely the reward for me, as the person in charge, with all the attendant headaches, at the Village Vanguard. A musician like that appears out of the blue, and our audience ate him up. Nobody had ever heard of him. (And nobody has seen him since, actually.) Didn't matter. The man played a ton of piano.

I confess I usually use up every musician that I love in fifty weeks and find myself left with two weeks—always in July or August, it seems—when I can't find anyone I really want. There are plenty of people I do not want. Virtually every musician I have dealt with, though, since taking over at the Vanguard, has been wonderful. I know this sounds saccharine but I sincerely mean it. There have only been a handful who turned out not to be worthy of the Vanguard. But I'm not going to mention their names here.

I always have my ears open for the new man, the next phase of jazz history, in a way. And yes, I guess they usually are men. Ninety-eight percent of the players at the Vanguard have been men. Dorothy Donegan, Mary Lou Williams, Helen Merrill, Geri Allen, Mary Stallings, and Carol Sloane—the women jazz musicians who have played the Vanguard, I can count on one and a half hands.

My greatest female catch was the woefully forgotten guitarist Mary Osborne, who'd disappeared from the jazz scene after her days as a child prodigy in the 1930s and '40s. I'd listened to Mary Osborne a lot as a kid and had been very proud to know there was this woman—this *girl*—out there swinging away.

Forty years later I read something about her and decided to find Mary Osborne. She was living out in California. I called her, told her who I was, and offered her a gig at the Village Vanguard. She didn't believe me! But I persevered. It's all about how you approach people and present your needs, your desires to them—for them. If they can connect to that, beautiful.

Turned out Mary was very sick, in the latter stages of cancer. But she did come to play in August 1991. She died the following year. Vanguard audiences were the last to hear her. I'm grateful for that.

I have never hired any women trumpet players or sax players. I know they exist. Maybe I just haven't heard enough. I grew up listening to men, mostly, playing jazz. There's something special about a man putting a tenor sax in his mouth and blowing it. It's a very sexy game, jazz.

*"She's maintained the integrity of the room.
It's a great feat, especially in our time,
when integrity is a curse word and
selling out a religion."*

—Wynton Marsalis

Trumpeter

Artistic director of Jazz at Lincoln Center

Preceding page: Alone at the Village Vanguard. My desk in the kitchen.

CHAPTER 16

AFTER LIFE AT THE VILLAGE VANGUARD

I COULD SIGN A HUNDRED-YEAR LEASE for the Vanguard any-time I want to, but I figure my current lease should outlast me and who cares after that. Let my daughter Deborah and her cohorts sign the next lease. It's in their hands—every-thing is set up for the next generation. My daughter knows a lot. She may not be as pushy as me, but that's all right. She'll do it her way.

It has taken seventy years for the Village Vanguard to grow and it's certainly not done yet. The whole scene was so different when Max started. For one thing, no one from the city came to inspect the place every five minutes in Max's day, like they do now, to see if the top is on the mayonnaise jar (and we don't even serve food). You didn't need a lot of money to run a club then. Rent was forty dollars a month. You didn't serve food, or maybe you did sometimes, when you felt like it. But the expenses were minimal.

It's very complicated to run the Village Vanguard today.

Max used to pay Miles Davis five hundred dollars a week. I just paid one young musician twenty-seven thousand dollars for one week. In fact, many of the Vanguard's greatest jazz names in the 1950s and 1960s did not do great business. Not at first. Eventually they got more notice and were recorded a lot, often at the Vanguard, and that contributed greatly to their growth, and to the club's. (At last count, more than a hundred albums have been recorded live at the Village Vanguard. And counting.)

I actually think jazz is more alive today than it has ever been in its hundred-plus-year history. There are so many more avenues for a jazz musician to take now, so many more places to play: Europe, cruises, festivals. All of the world is open to jazz. There are festivals in the most unlikely, distant places. Festivals! When I was growing up, there were no jazz festivals. Eventually there was Newport and that was it.

No, I think jazz is *very* strong at the moment. Hey, look, the records never sold in the quantities that pop music or some other junk does. That's not the role of jazz, though of course, I'd like it to be. I'd like people to listen to jazz more than some of the garbage they listen to. But that's not to be. And that's okay. Let it have an audience that is strong, that is devoted, that is relatively knowledgeable, and open to new sounds and new players.

The other day I found myself listening again to some of my earliest Blue Note Records—Teddy Bunn, J. C. Higginbotham, and Frankie Newton. I could have cried. *That* sound does *not* exist anymore. But that's the music that I grabbed on to as a kid, and that is the music that helps me, to this day, understand what the new kids in jazz are doing.

Many now come out of the best music conservatories—

Berklee and the like. But I'm still old-fashioned—I don't care what school they went to. What do you sound like, man? It's all about what I *hear*.

I was so starry-eyed about jazz musicians as a girl. I met Art Tatum at a rent party and thought I would pass out from the pleasure. It was a Harlem rent party—put a dollar in the bucket and go get yourself a drink and something to eat from the table. This was before Alfred. I must have been eighteen.

Clearly I was kind of pushy even then, because there was Tatum at the piano, and there I was, in short order, actually sitting on the piano bench beside him. I mean, how could I go to a rent party with Art Tatum at the piano and not get right up close to him?

If you loved the music, you loved the artists, the guys themselves, in that small enclave of jazz lovers. I became good friends with many musicians then. I do that to some degree today. A lot of the people who have played for me at the Vanguard have become my friends. The drummer Paul Motian and I eat dinner together every Sunday night when he's in town playing.

Meanwhile, I continue to live the life that Max lived for all those years when we were together. Do you believe it?

Honestly? I do believe it.

I started as a kid listening to jazz records. I followed the jazz thread throughout my growing up years until I married Alfred Lion of Blue Note Records, who was practically nobody then. Come on, we were both nobodies. And we worked together for seven years, recording, hanging out with musicians, hanging out at Birdland on Broadway. My life for seven years was nothing but music, morning, noon,

At the Newport Jazz Festival, July 1958.

and night—seven years of that. Unrelenting. Which led me to Max Gordon. And more years, many, many more years of music and nightlife, nightclubs. I guess I was just meant for this. I must have been. It takes a lot of stamina. And then to have two children, and to raise those kids. At least I hope I raised them. They grow, no matter what you do.

What I'm saying is, I didn't arrive at the Village Vanguard from out of the blue. I stuck to what I loved. That was my art. I'm not a musician; I'm not a singer; I'm not a painter; I'm not an actress. I'm none of those things. But throughout my life I followed the course of the music that I loved. I was not a musicologist. Nor was I a theoretician. I loved jazz. And what I loved was terrific. I'm very proud of what I loved. And that is what allowed me to take on the Vanguard and carry on what was started here and is certainly not finished here.

I'm forever thinking, My goodness! If I didn't have this what would I do? There are benches in the park across Sixth Avenue where I see these little old women sitting every day. There but for the grace of God go I.

I was never free in my life. Not until now. I left my mother's house as a teenager and got married immediately, leaving her house for one that I tried to make my home. Then I left that house and entered another, where I had children and did all the lovely things I'd always wanted to do. Everything I wanted to do, I did. But I never had freedom. I worked. Still, I never knew what it was to be on my own.

Now I finally am. I take care of myself. I pay for myself. I've got my own apartment in the Village, close to the club, but not too close.

I wouldn't know how to sit back. Retire? What's the point? Life is so beautiful when you're passionate about something, when you're committed. And not everyone is so lucky as I was. I *am* lucky. I fully realize that. Max left me this wonderful little club. Except he didn't actually leave it to me. It was there. So I took it. By the horns. And I shook it up.

I don't believe in mystical woogie-joogie-woogie stuff, but I do keep thinking that this is where I was destined to wind up all along. I believe it was all charted out for me from the beginning somehow. For the time I've been allotted here, I was just destined to end up where I am today.

And I like to think that Max would approve of what I've done with his place. In fact, I have to think that he is happy because I'm forever hearing this rapping coming through the Vanguard walls: "Okay! Good work, girl!"

"Thanks," I say. "But don't call me, 'girl,' Max. I'm a woman."

VILLAGE VANGUARD CHRONOLOGY: THE LORRAINE GORDON YEARS

BY BRIAN RUSHTON

BRIAN RUSHTON was one of Lorraine Gordon's longstanding friends. He particularly loved the Village Vanguard, and made it a labor of love to research the Vanguard's history. Working from New York Public Library microfilm collections, Brian Rushton painstakingly compiled as complete a record as anyone possibly could of every Vanguard booking going back to the very beginning. He then meticulously indexed and cross-referenced his findings—all the names, all the dates—handsomely printed the whole extraordinary enterprise as a bound book and presented it to Lorraine as a gift. Lorraine calls it simply "The Bible." Brian continued to update "The Bible" regularly, until cancer took him in 2005. The larger section on Max Gordon's Vanguard years, Lorraine intends to publish in an appropriate way one day soon. Meanwhile she's delighted to be able to share her part of "The Bible" dedicated to the memory of Brian Rushton, with profound thanks.

—Barry Singer

5/23/89 – 5/28/89	Tommy Flanagan Trio
5/30/89 – 6/4/89	Teddy Edwards Quartet
6/6/89 – 6/11/89	Richie Cole Quartet
6/13/89 – 6/18/89	Bobby Watson Quintet
6/20/89 – 6/25/89	Frank Morgan Quartet
6/27/89 – 7/2/89	John Hicks Quintet
7/4/89 – 7/9/89	Louis Hayes Quintet
7/11/89 – 7/16/89	Joe Henderson/Charlie Haden Trio
7/18/89 – 7/23/89	Buck Clayton Swing Band
7/25/89 – 7/30/89	Illinois Jacquet Big Band
8/10/89 – 8/6/89	Kenny Burrell Quartet*
8/8/89 – 8/13/89	David Murray Quartet
8/15/89 – 8/20/89	Geof Keezer Quartet
8/22/89 – 8/28/89	Bob Mintzer Big Band
8/29/89 – 9/3/89	Arthur Blythe Quartet
9/5/89 – 9/10/89	Harper Brothers Quintet*
9/12/89 – 9/17/89	George Adams Quartet
9/19/89 – 9/24/89	Bill Frisell Quartet
9/26/89 – 10/1/89	Steve Kuhn Trio
10/2/89	Cecil Taylor with the Feel Trio
10/3/89 – 10/8/89	Dorothy Donegan Trio
10/10/89 – 10/15/89	Geri Allen, Charlie Haden, Paul Motian
10/17/89 – 10/22/89	George Coleman Quartet
10/24/89 – 10/29/89	Michel Petrucciani Trio
10/31/89 – 11/5/89	Tony Williams Quintet
11/7/89 – 11/12/89	Buddy De Franco/Terry Gibbs Quintet
11/14/89 – 11/19/89	David "Fathead" Newman Quintet
11/21/89 – 11/26/89	Don Pullen Trio
11/28/89 – 12/3/89	Tom Harrell Quintet
12/5/89 – 12/10/89	Bobby Watson Quintet
12/12/89 – 12/17/89	Branford Marsalis Quartet

* Denotes a live recording was made of the performance. See Discography (p. 277).
** Tribute concert to Lorraine Gordon at 8 P.M. June 19, 2006, at the Isaac Stern Auditorium in Carnegie Hall.

12/19/89 – 12/24/89	Ralph Moore Quintet
12/26/89 – 12/31/89	Charlie Haden's Liberation Music Orchestra
1/2/90 – 1/7/90	Frank Morgan Quartet
1/9/90 – 1/14/90	Richard Davis Quintet
1/16/90 – 1/21/90	Louis Hayes Quintet
1/23/90 – 1/28/90	Mingus Dynasty Band
1/30/90 – 2/4/90	Kenny Barron Quintet
2/6/90 – 2/11/90	Randy Weston African Rhythms Trio
2/13/90 – 2/18/90	Buck Clayton's Swing Band
2/19/90 – 2/26/90	The Mel Lewis Jazz Orchestra
2/27/90 – 3/1/90	Shirley Horn Trio
3/2/90 – 3/4/90	Shirley Horn Trio (with Buck Hill)
3/6/90 – 3/11/90	Wynton Marsalis Septet*
3/13/90 – 3/18/90	David Murray Quartet
3/20/90 – 3/25/90	Nils Lan Doky Quartet (with Bill Evans)
3/27/90 – 4/1/90	Ray Anderson Quartet (with Amina Claudine Myers)
4/3/90 – 4/8/90	George Coleman Quartet
4/10/90 – 4/15/90	Roy Hargrove Sextet
4/17/90 – 4/22/90	Johnny Griffin Quartet
4/24/90 – 4/29/90	Jackie McLean Quartet
5/1/90 – 5/6/90	Tony Williams Quintet
5/8/90 – 5/13/90	Milt Jackson Quartet
5/15/90 – 5/20/90	Jim Hall Quartet
5/22/90 – 5/27/90	Bill Frisell Quartet
5/29/90 – 6/3/90	Dorothy Donegan Trio
6/5/90 – 6/10/90	Joe Henderson, Charlie Haden, AI Foster
6/12/90 – 6/17/90	Frank Wess Quartet
6/19/90 – 6/24/90	Charles McPherson Quartet
6/26/90 – 7/1/90	Bob Mintzer Big Band
7/3/90 – 7/8/90	Dewey Redman Quartet (with Geri Allen)
7/10/90 – 7/15/90	Don Pullen Trio
7/17/90 – 7/22/90	Kenny Burrell Quartet

7/24/90 – 7/29/90	David "Fathead" Newman Quintet
7/31/90 – 8/5/90	Bobby Hutcherson Quartet
8/7/90 – 8/12/90	Arthur Blythe Quintet
8/14/90 – 8/19/90	Shirley Horn Trio
8/21/90 – 8/26/90	Pharoah Sanders Quartet
8/28/90 – 9/2/90	Buster Williams Quintet
9/4/90 – 9/9/90	Mingus Dynasty Band
9/10/90	Bob Mintzer Big Band
9/11/90 – 9/16/90	Bobby Watson's Horizon Quintet
9/18/90 – 9/23/90	Harper Brothers Quintet
9/25/90 – 9/30/90	Randy Weston Trio
10/2/90 – 10/7/90	Kenny Barron Quintet
10/9/90 – 10/14/90	Geri Allen Quartet
10/16/90 – 10/21/90	Buck Clayton Swing Band
10/23/90 – 10/28/90	Roy Hargrove Quintet
10/30/90 – 11/4/90	Christian Escondé/Pierre Michelot Quartet*
11/6/90 – 11/9/90	Clark Terry Quartet
11/10/90 – 11/11/90	Buddy Tate Quartet
11/13/90 – 11/18/90	Henry Threadgill Septet
11/20/90 – 11/25/90	Don Pullen Trio
11/27/90 – 12/2/90	Tony Williams Quintet
12/4/90 – 12/9/90	Red Rodney Quintet
12/11/90 – 12/16/90	Jackie McLean Quartet
12/18/90 – 12/23/90	Geri Allen, Charlie Haden, Paul Motian*
12/25/90 – 12/30/90	Charlie Haden Liberation Music Orchestra
1/1/91 – 1/6/91	Larry Coryell Quartet
1/8/91 – 1/13/91	Geoff Keezer Quartet
1/15/91 – 1/20/91	Ed Blackwell Project
1/22/91 – 1/27/91	Shirley Horn Trio
1/29/91 – 2/1/91	Bobby Watson Horizon Quintet
2/5/91 – 2/10/91	Harry Connick Jr. Quartet
2/12/91 – 2/17/91	Kenny Barron Quintet

2/18/91	The Vanguard Jazz Orchestra [formerly the Mel Lewis Big Band] every Monday night hereon, except where otherwise listed.
2/19/91 – 2/24/91	Bill Frisell Quartet (with Don Byron)
2/26/91 – 3/3/91	Harper Brothers Quintet
3/5/91 – 3/10/91	Mark Whitfield Quartet
3/12/91 – 3/17/91	Mal Waldron Trio
3/18/91 – 3/21/91	The Vanguard Jazz Orchestra [twentieth anniversary]
3/22/91 – 3/24/91	Cecil Taylor
3/26/91 – 3/31/91	Butch Morris Ensemble
4/2/91 – 4/7/91	Branford Marsalis Trio
4/9/91 – 4/14/91	Johnny Griffin Quartet
4/16/91 – 4/21/91	Ray Anderson Quartet
4/23/91 – 4/28/91	Mingus Dynasty Band
4/30/91 – 5/5/91	Marlon Jordan Quintet
5/7/91 – 5/12/91	Charles McPherson Quartet
5/14/91 – 5/19/91	Jackie McLean Quintet
5/21/91 – 5/26/91	Dorothy Donegan Trio
5/28/91 – 6/2/91	Red Holloway Quartet
6/4/91 – 6/9/91	Barney Kessel Trio
6/11/91 – 6/16/91	David "Fathead" Newman Quintet (with James Clay)
6/18/91 – 6/23/91	Buster Williams Quintet
6/25/91 – 6/30/91	Tommy Flanagan Trio
7/2/91 – 7/7/91	Wynton Marsalis Septet*
7/9/91 – 7/14/91	Dewey Redman Quintet
7/16/91 – 7/21/91	Ralph Moore Quintet
7/23/91 – 7/28/91	Geri Allen Trio
7/30/91 – 8/4/91	Horace Tapscott Trio
8/6/91 – 8/11/91	Ed Blackwell Project
8/13/91 – 8/18/91	Harper Brothers Quintet
8/20/91 – 8/25/91	Joe Lovano Quintet
8/27/91 – 9/1/91	Mary Osborne Trio

9/3/91 – 9/8/91	Geoff Keezer Quartet
9/10/91 – 9/15/91	Arthur Blythe Quartet
9/17/91 – 9/22/91	Terence Blanchard Quintet
9/24/91 – 9/29/91	Johnny Griffin Quartet
10/1/91 – 10/6/91	Vincent Herring Quintet
10/8/91 – 10/13/91	Jay Hoggard Quartet
10/15/91 – 10/20/91	Jackie McLean Quintet
10/22/91 – 10/27/91	Pharoah Sanders Quartet
10/29/91 – 11/3/91	Shirley Horn Trio
11/5/91 – 11/10/91	Benny Green Trio*
11/12/91 – 11/17/91	Sun Ra All-Star Inventions*
11/19/91 – 11/24/91	Kenny Baron Quartet
11/25/91	Loren Schoenburg Big Band
11/26/91 – 12/1/91	Don Pullen Trio
12/3/91 – 12/8/91	Jim Hall Quartet
12/10/91 – 12/15/91	Barney Kessel Trio
12/17/91 – 12/22/91	Geri Allen, David Murray, Richard Davis, Andrew Cyrille
12/24/91 – 12/29/91	Roy Hargrove Quintet
12/31/91 – 1/5/92	Dr. Michael White's Original Liberty Jazz Band of New Orleans*
1/7/92 – 1/12/92	Danny Moore Quintet
1/14/92 – 1/19/92	Mundell Lowe Quartet
1/21/92 – 1/26/92	Walt Dickerson Trio
1/28/92 – 2/2/92	John Abercrombie Trio
2/4/92 – 2/9/92	Dorothy Donegan Trio
2/11/92 – 2/16/92	Joe Lovano Quartet (with Michel Petrucciani)
2/18/92 – 2/23/92	Grady Tate Quintet
2/25/92 – 3/1/92	Ray Anderson Quartet
3/3/92 – 3/8/92	Arthur Taylor's Wailers
3/10/92 – 3/15/92	Mal Waldron Trio
3/17/92 – 3/22/92	Ed Blackwell Project
3/24/92 – 3/29/92	Donald Harrison Quintet
3/31/92 – 4/5/92	McCoy Tyner Trio

4/7/92 – 4/12/92	Bradford Marsalis Trio
4/14/92 – 4/19/92	Butch Morris Ensemble
4/21/92 – 4/26/92	Terrance Blanchard Quintet
4/28/92 – 5/3/92	Max Roach Quartet
5/5/92 – 5/10/92	Johnny Griffin Quartet
5/12/92 – 5/17/92	Harper Brothers
5/19/92 – 5/24/92	Larry Coryell Quartet
5/26/92 – 5/31/92	Roy Hargrove Quintet
6/2/92 – 6/7/92	Mark Whitfield Trio
6/9/92 – 6/14/92	Don Cherry Quartet
6/16/92 – 6/21/92	Tommy Flanagan Trio
6/23/92 – 6/28/92	Ira Sullivan Quartet
6/30/92 – 7/5/92	Horace Tapscott Trio
7/7/92 – 7/12/92	Charles McPherson Quartet
7/14/92 – 7/19/92	Ahmad Jamal Trio
7/21/92 – 7/26/92	Dewey Redman Quartet
7/28/92 – 8/2/92	Jay Hoggard Quartet
8/4/92 – 8/9/92	David Murray Quartet (with Don Pullen)
8/11/92 – 8/16/92	Bill Frisell Band
8/18/92 – 8/23/92	Clark Terry Quintet
8/25/92 – 8/30/92	Arthur Taylor's Wailers*
9/1/92 – 9/4/92	Joshua Redman, Pat Metheny, Charlie Hadden, Billy Higgins*
9/5/92 – 9/6/92	Joshua Redman, Brad Mehldau, Ugoma Okegwo, Leon Parker
9/8/92 – 9/13/92	Javon Jackson, Kenny Baron, Ron Carter, Curtis Fuller, Lewis Nash
9/15/92 – 9/20/92	Bobby Watson and Horizon
9/22/92 – 9/27/92	Joe Lovano Quartet
9/29/92 – 10/4/92	Buster Williams Quintet
10/6/92 – 10/11/92	Ray Drummond Quintet
10/13/92 – 10/18/92	Pharoah Sanders Quartet
10/20/92 – 10/25/92	Geri Allen Trio*
10/27/92 – 11/1/92	Roy Haynes Quartet
11/3/92 – 11/8/92	Shirley Horn Trio

11/10/92 – 11/15/92	Illinois Jacquet Big Band
11/17/92 – 11/22/92	Roy Hargrove Quintet
11/24/92 – 11/29/92	Terence Blanchard Quintet
12/1/92 – 12/6/92	Toninho Horta, Gary Peacock, Billy Higgins
12/8/92 – 12/13/92	Jackie McLean Sextet
12/15/92 – 12/20/92	Benny Green Trio
12/22/92 – 12/27/92	Eastern Rebellion (Ralph Moore, Cedar Walton, David Williams, Billy Higgins)
12/29/92 – 1/3/93	Dr. Michael White's Original Liberty Jazz Band of New Orleans
1/5/93 – 1/10/93	Michel Petrucciani Quartet
1/12/93 – 1/17/93	Lou Donaldson Quartet
1/19/93 – 1/24/93	Larry Coryell Quartet
1/26/93 – 1/31/93	David Murray Quartet
2/2/93 – 2/7/93	Slide Hampton and the Jazzmasters
2/9/93 – 2/14/93	Tommy Flanagan Trio
2/16/93 – 2/21/93	Mulgrew Miller Trio
2/23/93 – 2/28/93	"The Message" (tribute to Art Blakey): Ralph Moore, Donald Harrison, Robin Eubanks, Brian Lynch, Geoff Keezer, Peter Washington, Carl Allen
3/2/93 – 3/7/93	Marcus Roberts Quartet
3/9/93 – 3/14/93	Mal Waldron Trio
3/16/93 – 3/21/93	George Coleman Quartet
3/23/93 – 3/28/93	Charles McPherson Quartet
3/30/93 – 4/4/93	Joshua Redman Quartet
4/6/93 – 4/11/93	Kenny Barron Trio with David Sanchez
4-7 P.M. 4/11/93	"Tribute to a Jazz Fan: Saxophones for Allison" with David Murray, George Coleman, Pharoah Sanders, John Stubblefield, Joe Lovano, John Hicks, et al
4/13/93 – 4/18/93	Kenny Barron Trio with Steve Nelson
4/20/93 – 4/25/93	Kenny Barron Trio with Gary Bartz
4/27/93 – 4/29/93	Bobby Watson and Horizon
4/30/93 – 5/2/93	Bobby Watson Tailor Made Band

5/4/93 – 5/9/93	Geri Allen Quartet
5/11/93 – 5/16/93	Terence Blanchard Quintet
5/18/3 – 5/23/93	Joe Lovano, Kenny Werner, Henri Texier, Aldo Romano
5/25/93 – 5/30/93	Don Pullen and the African-Brazilian Connection
6/1/93 – 6/6/93	Roy Haynes Quartet
6/8/93 – 6/13/93	Don Byron Quartet
6/15/93 – 6/20/93	Paul Motian/Joe Lovano/Bill Frisell Trio
6/22/93 – 6/27/93	Arthur Blythe Quartet*
6/29/93 – 7/4/93	Stephen Scott Trio (and special guests)
7/6/93 – 7/11/93	Pharoah Sanders Quartet
7/13/93 – 7/18/93	Shirley Scott Trio
7/20/93 – 7/25/93	Jimmy Heath Quartet
7/27/93 – 8/1/93	Mulgrew Miller Trio
8/3/93 – 8/8/93	Dorothy Donegan Trio
8/10/93 – 8/15/93	Ahmad Jamal Trio
8/17/93 – 8/22/93	David Murray Trio*
8/24/93 – 8/29/93	Kenny Burrell Quartet*
8/31/93 – 9/5/93	Billy Childs Trio
9/7/93 – 9/12/93	Ray Drummond Sextet
9/14/93 – 9/19/93	Lou Donaldson Quartet
9/21/93 – 9/26/93	Arthur Taylor's Wailers
9/28/93 – 10/3/93	Bill Frisell Trio
10/5/93 – 10/6/93	Pinetop Perkins, Charles "Honeyboy" Otis, Tom Pindell
10/7/93 – 10/10/93	Joshua Redman Quartet
10/12/93 – 10/17/93	Pharoah Sanders Quartet
10/19/93 – 10/24/93	Javon Jackson Quintet
10/26/93 – 10/31/93	George Coleman Quartet
11/2/93 – 11/7/93	Andrew Hill Quartet
11/9/93 – 11/14/93	Clark Terry Quintet
11/16/93 – 11/21/93	Danilo Perez Quintet
11/23/93 – 11/28/93	Vincent Herring Quintet*
11/30/93 – 12/5/93	Wynton Marsalis Sextet*

12/7/93 – 12/12/93	Jackie McLean Quintet
12/14/93 – 12/19/93	Roy Hargrove Quintet
12/21/93 – 12/26/93	Eastern Rebellion (Ralph Moore, Cedar Walton, David Williams, Billy Higgins)
12/28/93 – 1/2/94	Dr. Michael White's Original Liberty Jazz Band of New Orleans
1/4/94 – 1/9/94	Tommy Flanagan Trio
1/11/94 – 1/16/94	Arthur Blythe Quartet
1/18/94 – 1/23/94	Von Freeman Quartet
1/25/94 – 1/30/94	Cyrus Chestnut Trio
2/1/94 – 2/6/94	Lou Donaldson Quartet (with Dr. Lonnie Smith)
2/8/94 – 2/13/94	Lou Donaldson Quartet (with Dr. Lonnie Smith)
2/15/94 – 2/20/94	The Bluiett Four
2/22/94 – 2/27/94	Barry Harris Trio
3/1/94 – 3/6/94	John Byron Quintet
3/8/94 – 3/13/94	Joe Lovano Quartet
3/15/94 – 3/20/94	Bobby Hutcherson Quartet
3/22/94 – 3/27/94	Mal Waldron Trio
3/29/94 – 4/3/94	Art Farmer Quintet
4/5/94 – 4/10/94	Art Farmer Sextet
4/12/94 – 4/17/94	Pharoah Sanders Quartet
4/19/94 – 4/24/94	David Murray Quartet
4/26/94 – 5/1/94	George Coleman Quartet
5/3/94 – 5/8/94	Junko Onishi Trio*
5/10/94 – 5/15/94	Eastern Rebellion
5/17/94 – 5/22/94	Craig Handy Quartet
5/24/94 – 5/30/94	The Vanguard Jazz Orchestra [twenty-fifth anniversary]
5/31/94 – 6/5/94	David Sanchez Quartet
6/7/94 – 6/12/94	Paul Motian, Joe Lovano, Bill Frisell
6/14/94 – 6/19/94	Larry Coryell Trio
6/21/94 – 6/26/94	Cecil Taylor "Highpower Bullcult"
6/28/94 – 7/3/94	Mulgrew Miller Trio

7/5/94 – 7/10/94	Don Cherry Quartet
7/11/94	Loren Schoenberg Big Band
7/12/94 – 7/17/94	Barry Harris Trio
7/19/94 – 7/24/94	The Bluiett Four*
7/26/94 – 7/31/94	Marvin "Smitty" Smith Quartet
8/2/94 – 8/7/94	Wallace Roney Quintet
8/9/94 – 8/14/94	Lou Donaldson Quartet
8/16/94 – 8/21/94	Cyrus Chestnut Trio
8/23/94 – 8/28/94	Roy Haynes Quintet
8/30/94 – 9/4/94	Ruth Brown and Friends
9/6/94 – 9/11/94	Don Byron Quintet
9/13/94 – 9/18/94	Ron Carter Quintet
9/20/94 – 9/25/94	Kenny Barron, Buster Williams, Ben Riley (guest: Jesse Davis)
9/27/94 – 10/2/94	Kenny Barron, Buster Williams, Ben Riley (guest: Gary Bartz)
10/4/94 – 10/9/94	Kenny Barron, Buster Williams, Ben Riley (guest: James Spaulding)
10/11/94 – 10/16/94	Bobby Hutcherson Quartet
10/18/94 – 10/23/94	Joe Lovano "Universal Language"
10/25/94 – 10/30/94	Terence Blanchard Quartet
11/1/94 – 11/6/94	George Coleman Quartet
11/8/94 – 11/13/94	Benny Green Trio
11/15/94 – 11/20/94	Geri Allen Trio
11/22/94 – 11/27/94	Holly Hoffman Quartet
11/29/94 – 12/4/94	Wynton Marsalis Septet*
12/6/94 – 12/11/94	McCoy Tyner Trio
12/13/94 – 12/18/94	Clark Terry Quintet
12/20/94 – 12/25/94	Eastern Rebellion (Ralph Moore, Cedar Walton, David Williams, Billy Higgins)*
12/27/94 – 1/1/95	Dr. Michael White's Original Liberty Jazz Band of New Orleans
1/3/95 – 1/8/95	Ray Drummond Sextet
1/10/95 – 1/15/95	Tommy Flanagan Trio
1/17/95 – 1/22/95	Joe Lovano Quartet

1/24/95 – 1/29/95	Jacky Terrasson Trio
1/30/95 – 2/6/95	The Vanguard Jazz Orchestra
2/7/95 – 2/12/95	Art Farmer Quintet
2/14/95 – 2/19/95	Art Farmer Quintet
2/20/95 – 2/27/95	The Vanguard Jazz Orchestra

SIXTIETH-ANNIVERSARY APPEARANCES

2/21/95	Shirley Horn
2/22/95	Dick Gregory
2/23/95	Allen Ginsberg
2/24/95	Jimmy Rowles, Stacey Rowles, Bobby Short
2/25/95	Jimmy Rowles, Stacey Rowles, Irwin Corey
2/26/95	Pete Seeger
2/28/95 – 3/3/95	Stephen Scott Trio
3/4/95 – 3/5/95	Betty Carter Quintet
3/7/95 – 3/12/95	Christian McBride Quartet
3/14/95 – 3/19/95	Nicholas Payton Quintet
3/21/95 – 3/26/95	Joshua Redman Quartet*
3/28/95 – 4/2/95	Cecil Taylor Trio
4/4/95 – 4/9/95	Joe Lovano Quartet
4/11/95 – 4/16/95	Ron Carter Quintet
4/18/95 – 4/23/95	Geri Allen Trio
4/25/95 – 4/30/95	Harold Ashby Quartet (Dedicated to Duke Ellington)
5/2/95 – 5/7/95	David Sanchez Quartet
5/9/95 – 5/14/95	Bill Frisell Trio
5/16/95 – 5/21/95	Marcus Roberts Trio
5/23/95 – 5/28/95	Wessell Anderson/Wycliffe Gordon Quintette
5/30/95 – 6/4/95	Mal Waldron/Steve Lacy Duo
6/6/95 – 6/11/95	Paul Motian, Bill Frisell, Joe Lovano*

6/13/95 – 6/19/95	Herb Jeffries, Dick Katz, Peter Bernstein, Jamil Nassaer, Leroy Williams
6/27/95 – 7/2/95	Roy Hargrove Quintet
7/4/95 – 7/9/95	Jimmy Heath Quartet
7/11/95 – 7/16/95	Stanley Turrentine Quintet
7/18/95 – 7/23/95	Lou Donaldson Quartet
7/25/95 – 7/30/95	George Coleman Quartet
8/1/95 – 8/6/95	Slide Hampton and the Jazzmasters*
8/8/95 – 8/13/95	Cyrus Chestnut Trio
8/15/95 – 8/20/95	Wallace Roney Quintet
8/22/95 – 8/27/95	Tommy Flanagan Trio
8/29/95 – 9/3/95	Stephen Scott Trio
9/5/95 – 9/10/95	Clark Terry Quintet
9/12/95 – 9/17/95	Ron Carter Quintet
9/19/95 – 9/24/95	Benny Bailey Quartet
9/26/95 – 10/1/95	Jim Hall Trio
10/3/95 – 10/8/95	Ray Drummond Quintet
10/10/95 – 10/15/95	Geri Allen Trio
10/17/95 – 10/22/95	Pharoah Sanders Quartet
10/24/95 – 10/29/95	Harold Ashby Quartet
10/31/95 – 11/5/95	Dee Dee Bridgewater and Her Trio
11/7/95 – 11/12/95	Javon Jackson Quartet
11/14/95 – 11/19/95	Mark Whitfield Quartet
11/21/95 – 11/26/95	Lou Donaldson Quartet
11/28/95 – 12/3/95	James Carter Quartet
12/5/95 – 12/10/95	Bobby Hutcherson Quartet
12/12/95 – 12/17/95	Jackie McLean Sextet
12/19/95 – 12/24/95	Eastern Rebellion (Cedar Walton, David Williams, Kenny Washington, Vincent Herring)
12/26/95 – 12/31/95	Dr. Michael White's Original Liberty Jazz Band of New Orleans
1/2/95 – 1/7/95	Jeanie Bryson, Peter Berstein, Ted Brancato, Ray Drummond, Payton Crossley

1/9/96 – 1/14/96	Wessell Anderson/Wycliffe Gordon Quintet
1/16/96 – 1/21/96	Barry Harris Trio
1/23/96 – 1/28/96	Kenny Barron Trio
1/29/96	Roy Hargrove Big Band
1/30/96 – 2/6/96	The Vanguard Jazz Orchestra [thirtieth anniversary]
2/5/96	Roy Hargrove Big Band
2/6/96 – 2/11/96	Art Farmer Quintet
2/13/96 – 2/18/96	Art Farmer Quintet
2/20/96 – 2/25/96	Jacky Terrasson Trio
2/27/96 – 3/3/96	Holly Hofmann, Ray Brown, Kenny Barron, Victor Lewis
3/5/96 – 3/17/96	Tommy Flanagan Trio
3/19/96 – 3/21/96	Joe Lovano Quartet
3/26/96 – 3/31/96	Joe Lovano Quartet*
4/2/96 – 4/7/96	Roy Haynes Quartet
4/9/96 – 4/14/96	George Coleman Quartet
4/16/96 – 4/21/96	Christian McBride Quartet
4/23/96 – 4/28/96	Lou Donaldson Quartet
4/30/96 – 5/5/96	Jimmy Heath Quartet
5/7/96 – 5/12/96	Ron Carter Quintet
5/14/96 – 5/16/96	Larry Adler with Paulette Ivory
5/17/96 – 5/19/96	Jay McShann Quartet
5/21/96 – 5/26/96	Harold Ashby Quartet
5/28/96 – 6/2/96	Nicholas Payton Quintet
6/4/96 – 6/6/96	Roy Hargrove Quintet
6/7/96 – 6/9/96	Roy Hargrove Big Band with Miguel "Anga" Diaz
6/11/96 – 6/16/96	James Carter Quartet
6/18/96 – 6/23/96	Marcus Roberts Trio
6/25/96 – 6/30/96	Benny Bailey Quartet
7/2/96 – 7/7/96	Jackie McLean Sextet
7/9/96 – 7/14/96	Jeanie Bryson and her Quintet
7/16/96 – 7/21/96	Wessell Anderson Quintet

7/23/96 – 7/28/96	Branford Marsalis Trio
7/30/96 – 8/4/96	Lou Donaldson Quartet
8/6/96 – 8/11/96	Geri Allen Trio
8/13/96 – 8/18/96	Eric Reed Trio
8/20/96 – 8/25/96	Terence Blanchard Quintet
8/27/96 – 9/1/96	Wycliffe Gordon/Ronald Westray Quintet
9/3/96 – 9/8/96	Clark Terry Quintet
9/10/96 – 9/15/96	Ron Carter Quintet
9/17/96 – 9/22/96	Paul Motian, Bill Frisell, Joe Lovano
9/24/96 – 9/29/96	Roy Hargrove Big Band
10/1/96 – 10/6/96	Javon Jackson Quartet
10/8/96 – 10/13/96	Ray Drummond Quintet
10/15/96 – 10/20/96	Ron Affif Trio
10/22/96 – 10/27/96	Wallace Roney Quintet
10/29/96 – 11/3/96	David Sanchez Quintet
11/4/96 – 11/10/96	Roy Haynes Quartet
11/12/96 – 11/17/96	Cyrus Chestnut Trio
11/19/96 – 11/24/96	George Coleman Quartet
11/26/96 – 12/1/96	Tommy Flanagan Trio
12/3/96 – 12/8/96	Jim Hall Trio (guests: Kenny Barron, Slide Hampton, Greg Osby, Art Farmer, Geoff Keezer)*
12/10/96 – 12/15/96	Jackie McLean Sextet
12/17/96 – 12/22/96	Kenny Barron Quartet
12/24/96 – 12/29/96	Cedar Walton Quartet
12/31/96 – 1/5/97	Dr. Michael White's Original Liberty Jazz Band of New Orleans
1/7/97 – 1/12/97	Jackie McLean with the Cedar Walton Trio
1/14/97 – 1/19/97	Lou Donaldson Quartet
1/21/97 – 1/26/97	Wycliffe Gordon/Ronald Westray Quartet
1/28/97 – 2/2/97	Brad Mehldau Trio
2/4/97 – 2/9/97	Bobby Hutcherson Quartet
2/11/97 – 2/16/97	Larry Smith Quartet

2/18/97 – 2/23/97	Benny Green and the "Kaleidoscope" Band
2/24/97 – 3/2/97	The Vanguard Jazz Orchestra [thirty-first anniversary]
3/3/97	Loren Schoenberg Big Band
3/4/97 – 3/16/97	Tommy Flanagan Trio*
3/18/97 – 3/23/97	Ron Affif Trio
3/25/97 – 3/30/97	Buster Williams Quartet
4/1/97 – 4/6/97	Roy Hargrove Sextet
4/7/97	Roy Hargrove Big Band
4/8/97 – 4/13/97	David Sanchez Quintet
4/15/97 – 4/20/97	Wessell Anderson Quintet
4/22/97 – 4/27/97	Charles McPherson Quartet
4/29/97 – 5/4/97	Barry Harris Trio
5/6/97 – 5/11/97	Ron Carter Quintet
5/13/97 – 5/18/97	Stanley Turrentine Quintet
5/20/97 – 5/25/97	The Heath Brothers
5/27/97 – 6/1/97	Lou Donaldson Quartet
6/3/97 – 6/8/97	Ray Drummond Quartet
6/10/97 – 6/15/97	Harold Ashby Quartet
6/17/97 – 6/22/97	Jim Hall Quartet
6/24/97 – 6/29/97	Christian McBride Quartet
7/1/97 – 7/6/97	Leroy Jones Quintet
7/8/97 – 7/13/97	Bill Frisell Quartet
7/15/97 – 7/20/97	Fred Hersch Trio
7/22/97 – 7/27/97	Kenny Barron Trio
7/29/97 – 8/3/97	Brad Mehldau Trio*
8/5/97 – 8/10/97	Cecil Taylor Trio
8/12/97 – 8/17/97	Geri Allen Trio
8/19/97 – 8/24/97	Cyrus Chestnut Trio
8/26/97 – 8/31/97	Clark Terry Quintet
9/2/97 – 9/7/97	Tommy Flanagan Trio
9/9/97 – 9/14/97	Tommy Flanagan Trio
9/16/97 – 9/21/97	Paul Motian, Joe Lovano, Bill Frisell*

JOHN COLTRANE BIRTHDAY CELEBRATION

9/23/97	McCoy Tyner Trio*
9/24/97	Danilo Perez Trio
9/25/97	Antonio Hart Quartet
9/26/97	Eric Reed Trio
9/27/97	Donald Harrison Quartet
9/28/97	Diana Krall, Russell Malone, Christian McBride
9/30/97 – 10/5/97	Marcus Roberts Twelve-Piece Band
10/7/97 – 10/12/97	Charles McPherson Quartet
10/14/97 – 10/19/97	Lou Donaldson Quartet
10/21/97 – 10/26/97	Bobby Hutcherson Quartet
10/28/97 – 11/2/97	Russell Malone Quartet
11/4/97 – 11/9/97	Winard Harper Quintet
11/11/97 – 11/16/97	Eric Reed Trio
11/18/97 – 11/23/97	Buster Williams Quartet
11/25/97 – 11/30/97	"Trio" featuring Joshua Redman, Christian McBride, Brian Blade
12/2/97 – 12/7/97	Joe Lovano Quartet
12/9/97 – 12/14/97	Nicholas Payton Quintet
12/16/97 – 12/21/97	Jackie McLean with the Cedar Walton Trio
12/23/97 – 12/28/97	Cedar Walton Quartet
12/30/97 – 1/4/98	Dr. Michael White's Original Liberty Jazz Band of New Orleans
1/6/98 – 1/7/98	Joe Lovano Quartet
1/8/98 – 1/9/98	Joe Lovano Ensemble, "Celebrating Sinatra"
1/10/98 – 1/11/98	Joe Lovano with Gonzalo Rubalcaba
1/13/98 – 1/18/98	Donald Harrison Quartet
1/20/98 – 1/25/98	Roy Hargrove Sextet
1/27/98 – 2/1/98	Fred Hersch Trio
2/3/98 – 2/8/98	Barry Harris Trio
2/10/98 – 2/15/98	Ron Carter Quintet

2/17/98 – 2/22/98	Ron Carter Sextet with Houston Person
2/23/98	Youth Big Band [before the Vanguard Jazz Orchestra]
2/24/98 – 3/1/98	James Carter Quartet
3/3/98 – 3/8/98	Tom Harrell Septet
3/10/98 – 3/15/98	Brad Mehldau Trio
3/17/98 – 3/29/98	Tommy Flanagan Trio
3/31/98 – 4/5/98	David Sanchez Quintet
4/7/98 – 4/12/98	Javon Jackson Quartet
4/14/98 – 4/19/98	Sphere
4/21/98 – 4/26/98	Leon Parker Quartet
4/28/98 – 5/3/98	Harold Ashby Quartet
5/5/98 – 5/10/98	Houston Person and Etta Jones
5/12/98 – 5/17/98	Buster Williams Quartet
5/19/98 – 5/24/98	Lou Donaldson Quartet
5/26/98 – 5/31/98	Wessell Anderson Quintet*
6/1/98 – 6/8/98	The Vanguard Jazz Orchestra
6/9/98	Edsel Gomez, John Benitez, Adam Cruz, Pernell Saturnino
6/10/98 – 6/14/98	Chucho Valdés and Trio
6/16/98 – 6/21/98	Ray Drummond Quartet
6/22/98 – 6/24/98	The Vanguard Jazz Orchestra
6/25/98 – 6/28/98	Shirley Horn Trio
6/30/98 – 7/5/98	Joe Lovano Quartet
7/7/98 – 7/12/98	Cedar Walton Trio
7/14/98 – 7/19/98	Roy Hargrove Sextet
7/20/98	Roy Hargrove Big Band
7/21/98 – 7/26/98	Winard Harper Quintet
7/28/98 – 8/2/98	Charles McPherson Quartet
8/4/98 – 8/9/98	Wycliffe Gordon Quintet
8/11/98 – 8/16/98	"Jazz Meets Flamenco" with Gil Goldstein, Jorge Pardo, Charles Benavant, Alea Acuňa
8/18/98 – 8/23/98	Geri Allen Sextet
8/25/98 – 8/30/98	Fred Hersch Trio

09/1/9 – 9/6/98	Barry Harris Trio
9/8/98 – 9/20/98	Tommy Flanagan Trio
9/22/98 – 9/27/98	David Sanchez Quintet
9/29/98 – 10/4/98	Russell Malone Quartet
10/6/98 – 10/11/98	Roy Haynes Quartet
10/13/98 – 10/18/98	Lewis Nash Septet
10/20/98 – 10/25/98	Lou Donaldson Quartet
10/27/98 – 11/1/98	Cyrus Chestnut Trio
11/3/98 – 11/8/98	The Heath Brothers
11/10/98 – 11/15/98	Leon Parker & Company
11/17/98 – 11/22/98	Marcus Roberts Trio
11/24/98 – 11/29/98	Clark Terry Quintet
12/1/98 – 12/6/98	Sphere
12/8/98 – 12/13/98	Houston Person and Etta James
12/15/98 – 12/20/98	Jackie McLean and the Cedar Walton Trio
12/22/98 – 12/27/98	Cedar Walton Trio
12/29/98 – 1/3/99	Dr. Michael White's Original Liberty Jazz Band of New Orleans
1/5/99 – 1/10/99	Brad Mehldau Trio*
1/12/99 – 1/17/99	"Trio Fascination" (Joe Lovano, Cameron Brown, Idris Muhammad)
1/19/99 – 1/24/99	Sherman Irby Quartet
1/26/99 – 1/31/99	The Vanguard Jazz Orchestra
2/2/99 – 2/7/99	Ray Drummond's All-Star Excursion Band
2/9/99 – 2/14/99	Roy Hargrove Sextet
2/16/99 – 2/21/99	Buster Williams Quartet
2/23/99 – 2/28/99	Barry Harris Trio
3/2/99 – 3/7/99	Tom Harrell Quintet
3/9/99 – 3/21/99	Tommy Flanagan Trio
3/23/99 – 3/28/99	Jim Hall Trio
3/30/99 – 4/11/99	Chucho Valdés Quintet*
4/13/99 – 4/18/99	Johnny Griffin Quartet
4/20/99 – 4/25/99	Lou Donaldson Quartet
4/27/99 – 5/2/99	The Heath Brothers
5/4/99 – 5/9/99	Branford Marsalis Quartet

5/11/99 – 5/16/99	Mark Turner Quartet
5/18/99 – 5/23/99	Bill Frisell Trio
5/25/99 – 5/30/99	Wycliffe Gordon Quintet
6/1/99 – 6/6/99	Teri Thornton Quintet
6/8/99 – 6/13/99	Joe Lovano Quintet
6/15/99 – 6/20/99	Fred Hersch Trio
6/22/99 – 6/27/99	Geri Allen Trio
6/29/99 – 7/11/99	Kenny Barron Trio
7/13/99 – 7/18/99	Kenny Drew Jr. Trio
7/20/99 – 7/25/99	Houston Person and Etta Jones
7/27/99 – 8/1/99	Chris Potter Quartet
8/3/99 – 8/8/99	Lou Donaldson Quartet
8/10/99 – 8/15/99	Lewis Nash Septet
8/17/99 – 8/22/99	Sherman Irby Quartet
8/24/99 – 8/29/99	Eric Reed's New York Seven
8/31/99 – 9/5/99	Tom Harrell Quintet
9/7/99 – 9/12/99	Clark Terry Quintet
9/14/99 – 9/26/99	Tommy Flanagan Trio
9/28/99 – 10/3/99	Cyrus Chestnut Trio
10/5/99 – 10/10/99	Russell Malone Quartet
10/12/99 – 10/17/99	Fred Hirsch Quintet
10/19/94 – 10/24/99	Stefon Harris Quartet
10/26/99 – 10/31/99	Geri Allen Trio
11/2/99 – 11/7/99	Regina Carter Sextet
11/9/99 – 11/14/99	Mary Stallings with the Eric Reed Trio
11/16/99 – 11/21/99	Houston Person and Etta Jones
11/23/99 – 11/28/99	Brad Mehldau Trio
11/30/99 – 12/5/99	Sphere
12/7/99 – 12/12/99	David Sanchez Sextet
12/14/99 – 12/19/99	Jackie McLean with the Cedar Walton Trio
12/21/99 – 12/26/99	Cedar Walton Quartet with Vincent Herring and Billy Higgins
12/28/99 – 1/2/00	Dr. Michael White's Original Liberty Jazz Band of New Orleans

1/3/00 – 1/9/00	Wynton Marsalis Septet
1/11/00 – 1/16/00	Kenny Drew Jr. Trio
1/18/00 – 1/23/00	Teri Thornton Sextet
1/25/00 – 1/30/00	Barry Harris Trio
2/1/00 – 2/6/00	Buster Williams Quintet
2/8/00 – 2/13/00	Charles McPherson Quartet
2/15/00 – 2/20/00	Roy Hargrove Quintet
2/22/00 – 2/27/00	Mark Turner Quartet
2/29/00 – 3/5/00	Dave Douglas Sextet
3/7/00 – 3/12/00	The Heath Brothers
3/14/00 – 3/26/00	Tommy Flanagan Trio
3/28/00 – 4/9/00	Lou Donaldson Quartet
4/11/00 – 4/16/00	Terence Blanchard Sextet
4/18/00 – 4/23/00	Geri Allen Trio
4/25/00 – 4/30/00	Joshua Redman Quartet
5/2/00 – 5/7/00	Johnny Griffin Quartet
5/9/00 – 5/14/00	Houston Person and Etta Jones
5/16/00 – 5/21/00	Joe Lovano Nonet
5/23/00 – 5/28/00	Wycliffe Gordon Quintet
5/30/00 – 6/4/00	Eric Reed's New York Seven
6/6/00 – 6/11/00	Leon Parker Quintet
6/13/00 – 6/18/00	Bobby Hutcherson Quartet
6/20/00 – 6/25/00	Brian Blade Fellowship
6/27/00 – 7/2/00	Kenny Drew Jr. Trio
7/4/00 – 7/9/00	Fred Hersch Trio
7/11/00 – 7/16/00	Jane Monheit Quintet
7/18/00 – 7/23/00	Gary Bartz Sextet
7/25/00 – 7/30/00	David "Fathead" Newman Quartet
8/1/00 – 8/6/00	Cedar Walton Trio
8/8/00 – 8/13/00	New Directions, featuring Mark Shim, Greg Osby, Jason Moran
8/15/00 – 8/20/00	Charles McPherson Quintet
8/22/00 – 8/27/00	Clark Terry Quintet
8/29/00 – 9/3/00	Jacky Terrasson Quartet
9/5/00 – 9/17/00	Tommy Flanagan Trio

9/19/00 – 9/24/00	Brad Mehldau Trio*
9/26/00 – 10/1/00	Mary Stallings with Eric Reed Trio*
10/3/00 – 10/8/00	Tom Harrell Quintet
10/10/00 – 10/15/00	Kenny Barron Trio
10/17/00 – 10/22/00	Lou Donaldson Quartet
10/24/00 – 10/29/00	Sherman Irby Quartet
10/31/00 – 11/5/00	Eric Alexander Quartet
11/7/00 – 11/12/00	Stefon Harris Quintet
11/14/00 – 11/19/00	Bill Charlap Trio
11/21/00 – 11/26/00	Roy Haynes Quartet
11/28/00 – 12/3/00	Bill Frisell Trio
12/5/00 – 12/7/00	Clark Terry Quintet
12/8/00 – 12/10/00	Roy Hargrove Quintet
12/12/00 – 12/17/00	Jackie McLean with Cedar Walton Trio
12/19/00 – 12/24/00	Cedar Walton Quartet
12/26/00 – 12/31/00	Dr. Michael White's Original Liberty Jazz Band of New Orleans
1/2/01 – 1/7/01	Buster Williams Quartet
1/9/01 – 1/14/01	Terence Blanchard Sextet
1/16/01 – 1/21/01	Jeff "Tain" Watts Quintet
1/23/01 – 1/28/01	Kurt Rosenwinkel Quartet
1/30/01 – 2/4/01	Ray Drummond Quartet
2/6/01 – 2/11/01	The Heath Brothers
2/13/01 – 2/18/01	Dave Douglas Quintet
2/20/01 – 2/25/01	An Evening with Branford Marsalis
2/27/01 – 3/4/01	Gary Bartz Quintet
3/6/01 – 3/11/01	Russell Malone Quartet
3/13/01 – 3/25/01	Tommy Flanagan Trio
3/27/01 – 4/1/01	Danilo Perez and the Motherland Project
4/3/01 – 4/8/01	Bobby Hutcherson Quartet
4/10/01 – 4/15/01	Chucho Valdés Quartet
4/17/01 – 4/22/01	Jim Hall Quartet
4/24/01 – 4/29/01	Louis Stewart Quartet
5/1/01 – 5/6/01	Jane Monheit Quintet

5/8/01 – 5/13/01	Houston Person and Etta Jones
5/15/01 – 5/20/01	Terence Blanchard Quintet
5/22/01 – 5/27/01	Mark Turner Quartet
5/29/01 – 6/3/01	Joe Lovano, "Flights of Fancy"
6/5/01 – 6/10/01	Leon Parker Quartet
6/12/01 – 6/17/01	Bill Charlap Trio
6/19/01 – 6/24/01	Tom Harrell Septet
6/26/01 – 7/1/01	Lewis Nash Septet
7/3/01 – 7/8/01	Lou Donaldson Quartet
7/10/01 – 7/15/01	David "Fathead" Newman Quartet
7/17/01 – 7/22/01	Fred Hersch Trio
7/24/01 – 7/29/01	Steve Wilson "Generations"
8/01/01 – 8/05/01	Greg Osby Four
8/07/01 – 8/12/01	Kurt Rosenwinkel Quartet
8/14/01 – 8/19/01	Jacky Terrasson Trio
8/21/01 – 8/26/01	Paul Motian, Bill Frisell, Joe Lovano
8/28/01 – 9/2/01	Charles McPherson Quartet
9/4/01 – 9/9/01	Regina Carter and Kenny Barron Duo
9/14/01 – 9/16/01	Tommy Flanagan Trio
9/18/01 – 9/23/01	Martial Solal Trio
9/25/01 – 9/30/01	Mary Stallings with George Cables Trio
10/2/01 – 10/7/01	Bill Frisell Trio
10/9/01 – 10/14/01	Bill Frisell Quartet
10/16/01 – 10/21/01	David Sanchez Quintet
10/23/01 – 10/28/01	Eric Alexander Quartet
10/30/01 – 11/4/01	Cyrus Chestnut Trio
11/6/01 – 11/11/01	Lou Donaldson Quartet
11/13/01 – 11/18/01	Tom Harrell Quintet
11/20/01 – 11/25/01	Brad Mehldau Trio
11/27/01 – 12/2/01	Greg Osby Five
12/4/01 – 12/9/01	Geri Allen Quartet
12/11/01 – 12/16/01	Bill Charlap Trio
12/18/01 – 12/23/01	Cedar Walton Trio with Jackie McLean
12/25/01 – 12/30/01	Cedar Walton Quartet

12/31/01 – 1/5/02	Dr. Michael White's Original Liberty Jazz Band of New Orleans
1/8/02 – 1/13/02	Buster Williams Quartet
1/15/02 – 1/20/02	Jeff "Tain" Watts Quintet
1/25/02 – 1/27/02	Don Byron Music for Six Musicians
1/29/02 · 2/3/02	Kenny Drew Jr. Trio
2/5/02 – 2/10/02	Mulgrew Miller Trio
2/12/02 – 2/17/02	Clark Terry Quintet
2/19/02 – 2/24/02	Bruce Barth Trio
2/26/02 – 3/3/02	Ray Drummond Quartet
3/5/02 – 3/17/02	Roy Hargrove Quintet
3/19/02 – 3/24/02	Carol Sloane, Norman Simmons, Paul West, Paul Bollenback, Winard Harper
3/26/02 – 3/31/02	Mark Turner Quartet
4/02/02 – 4/7/02	Eric Alexander Quintet
4/09/02 – 4/14/02	Steve Wilson Quartet
4/16/02 – 4/21/02	Barry Harris Trio
4/23/02 – 5/5/02	Lou Donaldson Quartet (featuring Dr. Lonnie Smith)
507/02 – 5/12/02	Cedar Walton Quartet
5/14/02 – 5/19/02	Fred Hersch Trio
5/21/02 – 5/26/02	Dave Douglas New Quintet
5/28/02 – 6/2/02	Tom Harrell Quintet
6/4/02 – 6/9/02	Jacky Terrasson Trio
6/11/02 – 6/16/02	Jim Hall Trio
6/18/02 – 6/23/02	Kurt Rosenwinkel Quartet

JVC JAZZ FESTIVAL

6/24/02	The Vanguard Jazz Orchestra with Joe Lovano
6/25/02	The Bad Plus with Ethan Iverson, Reid Anderson, Dave King
6/26/02	Don Byron Music for Six Musicians
6/27/02	Mark Turner Trio
6/28/02	Dave Douglas New Quintet

6/29/02 – 6/30/02	Jason Moran Trio
7/2/02 – 7/7/02	Gary Bartz Quintet
7/9/02 – 7/14/02	Buster Williams Quartet
7/16/02 – 7/21/02	Mulgrew Miller Trio
7/23/02 – 7/28/02	Larry Willis Trio
7/30/02 – 8/4/02	Bruce Barth Trio
8/6/02 – 8/11/02	Dianne Reeves
8/13/02 – 8/18/02	Bill Frisell Trio
8/20/02 – 8/25/02	Paul Motian, Bill Frisell, Joe Lovano
8/27/02 – 9/1/02	Don Byron Music for Six Musicians
9/3/02 – 9/8/02	Mary Stallings with the Eric Reed Trio
9/10/02 – 9/15/02	Bill Charlap Trio
9/17/02 – 9/22/02	Ted Nash's Odeon (featuring Wycliffe Gordon)
9/24/02 – 9/29/02	Joe Lovano Nonet
10/1/02 – 10/6/02	Brad Mehldau Trio
10/8/02 – 10/13/02	Jim Hall Quartet (featuring Greg Osby)
10/15/02 – 10/20/02	Bobby Henderson Quartet
10/22/02 – 10/27/02	Kenny Barron Sextet
10/29/02 – 11/3/02	Regina Carter Quintet
11/5/02 – 11/10/02	Greg Osby Quartet
11/12/02 – 11/17/02	Clark Terry Quintet
11/19/02 – 11/24/02	Lou Donaldson Quartet
11/26/02 – 12/1/02	Jason Moran Trio*
12/3/02 – 12/8/02	Geri Allen Trio
12/10/02 – 12/15/02	Chris Potter Quartet
12/17/02 – 12/22/02	Cedar Walton Trio with Vincent Herring
12/24/02 – 12/29/02	Cedar Walton Quartet
12/31/02 – 1/5/03	Dr. Michael White's Original Liberty Jazz Band of New Orleans
1/7/03 – 1/12/03	Paul Motian's Electric Bebop Band
1/14/03 – 1/26/03	Roy Hargrove Quintet
1/28/03 – 2/2/03	Fred Hersch Trio
2/4/03 – 2/9/03	Jacky Terrasson Trio

2/11/03 – 2/16/03   The Bad Plus (Ethan Iverson, Reid Anderson, Dave King)

2/18/03 – 2/23/03   Mark Turner Quartet

2/25/03 – 3/4/03   Joe Lovano Quartet [a special week dedicated to Dexter Gordon]

3/4/03 – 3/9/03   Kurt Rosenwinkel Quartet

3/11/03 – 3/16/03   Eric Reed Septet

3/18/03 – 3/23/03   Bill Charlap Trio

3/25/03 – 3/30/03   Eric Alexander Quintet

4/1/03 – 4/6/03   The Heath Brothers

4/8/03 – 4/13/03   Buster Williams Quintet

4/15/03 – 4/20/03   Don Byron Sextet

4/22/03 – 4/27/03   Jeremy Pelt Quintet

4/29/03 – 5/4/03   Tom Harrell Quintet

5/6/03 – 5/11/03   Barry Harris Trio

5/13/03 – 5/18/03   Ted Nash and Odeon

5/20/03 – 5/25/03   Uri Caine Trio*

5/27/03 – 6/1/03   Lou Donaldson Quartet

6/3/03 – 6/8/03   Jim Hall Trio

6/10/03 – 6/15/03   Wycliffe Gordon Quartet

6/17/03 – 6/22/03   Gary Bartz

JVC JAZZ FESTIVAL

6/23/03   The Vanguard Jazz Orchestra with Jimmy Heath

6/24/03   Tethered Moon with Masabumi Kikuchi, Gary Peacock, and Paul Motian

6/25/03   Marilyn Crispell with Mark Helias and Paul Motian

6/26/03   Bill McHenry Group with Duane Eubanks, Ethan Iverson, Reid Anderson, Ben Monder, and Paul Motian

6/27/03   Paul Motian's Electric Bebop Band with Tony Malaby, Chris Cheek, Ben Monder, Steve Cardenas, and Jerome Harris

6/28/03   Trio 2000 plus 1 with Tony Malaby, Drew Gress, Masabumi Kikuchi, and Paul Motian

7/1/03 – 7/6/03	Jerry Dodgion and the Joy of Sax
7/8/03 – 7/13/03	Renee Rosnes Quartet
7/15/03 – 7/20/03	Cedar Walton Quartet
7/22/03 – 7/27/03	Mark Turner/Ethan Iverson Quartet
7/29/03 – 8/3/03	Marcus Roberts Trio
8/5/03 – 8/10/03	Roy Hargrove Quintet
8/12/03 – 8/17/03	Larry Coryell
8/19/03 – 8/24/03	Fred Hersch Trio*
8/26/03 – 8/31/03	Paul Motian, Joe Lovano, Bill Frisell
9/2/03 – 9/7/03	Paul Motian, Joe Lovano, Bill Frisell
9/9/03 – 9/14/03	Harry Allen/Scott Hamilton Quintet
9/16/03 – 9/21/03	The Bad Plus
9/23/03 – 9/28/03	Joe Lovano Nonet
9/30/03 – 10/5/03	Jason Moran and the Bandwagon
10/7/03 – 10/12/03	Greg Osby Quartet
10/14/03 – 10/19/03	Eric Reed's New York Seven
10/21/03 – 10/26/03	Dave Douglas Sextet
10/28/03 – 11/2/03	Brad Mehldau Trio
11/4/03 – 11/09/03	Tom Harrell Quintet
11/11/03 – 11/16/03	Bill Charlap Trio
11/18/03 – 11/23/03	Kenny Barron Sextet
11/25/03 – 11/30/03	Lou Donaldson Quartet
12/2/03 – 12/07/03	Bill Frisell Trio
12/09/03 – 12/14/03	Bill Frisell Trio
12/16/03 – 12/21/03	Roy Hargrove with the Cedar Walton Trio
12/23/03 – 12/28/03	Cedar Walton Quartet with Vincent Herring
12/30/03 – 1/4/04	Chucho Valdés Quartet
1/6/04 – 1/11/04	Wessell Anderson Quintet with Wynton Marsalis
1/13/04 – 1/18/04	Carol Sloane
1/20/04 – 1/25/04	Terence Blanchard Sextet
1/27/04 – 2/1/04	Don Byron Quartet
2/3/04 – 2/8/04	Dave Douglas Quintet

2/10/04 – 2/15/04	Fly (Mark Turner, Larry Grenadier, Jeff Ballard)
2/17/04 – 2/22/04	Jacky Terrasson Trio
2/24/04 – 2/29/04	Barry Harris Trio
3/2/04 – 3/7/04	Eric Reed Quintet
3/9/04 – 3/14/04	Paul Motian's Electric Bebop Band
3/16/04 – 3/21/04	Jeff (Tain) Watts Quartet
3/23/04 – 3/28/04	Fred Hersch Trio + 2
3/30/04 – 4/4/04	Jerry Dodgion and the Joy of Sax
4/6/4 – 4/11/04	Bill Charlap Trio
4/13/04 – 4/18/04	Bill Charlap Trio
4/20/04 – 4/25/04	Steve Wilson Quartet
4/27/04 – 5/2/04	Jim Hall Trio
5/4/04 – 5/9/04	Clark Terry Quintet
5/11/04 – 5/16/04	Wycliffe Gordon Quintet
5/18/04 – 5/23/04	Chris Potter Group
5/25/04 – 5/30/04	Bill McHenry Quartet
6/1/04 – 6/6/04	Lou Donaldson Quartet
6/8/04 – 6/13/04	Marcus Roberts Trio
6/15/04 – 6/20/04	Greg Osby Quartet
6/22/04 – 6/27/04	Uri Caine (JVC Jazz Festival)
6/29/04 – 7/4/04	Tom Harrell Quintet
7/06/04 – 7/11/04	Mulgrew Miller Trio
7/13/04 – 7/18/04	Jeremy Pelt
7/20/04 – 7/25/04	Lewis Nash Quintet
7/27/04 – 8/1/04	Ben Riley's Monk Legacy Band
8/3/04 – 8/8/04	Al Foster Quartet
8/10/04 – 8/15/04	Joey Baron's Killer Joey
8/17/04 – 8/22/04	Cedar Walton Trio
8/24/04 – 8/29/04	Paul Motian/Joe Lovano/Bill Frisell Trio
8/31/04 – 9/5/04	Paul Motian/Joe Lovano/Bill Frisell Trio
9/7/04 – 9/12/04	Kenny Barron Sextet
9/14/04 – 9/19/04	Fly (Mark Turner, Larry Grenadier, Jeff Ballard)
9/21/04 – 9/26/04	The Bad Plus

9/28/04 – 10/3/04	Brad Mehldau Quartet
10/5/04 – 10/10/04	Roy Hargrove Quintet
10/12/04 – 10/17/04	Eric Reed Quintet
10/19/04 – 10/24/04	Jim Hall and Geoff Keezer
10/26/04 – 10/31/04	Charlie Haden Quintet
11/2/04 – 11/7/04	Bill McHenry Quartet
11/9/04 – 11/14/04	Joe Lovano Nonet
11/16/04 – 11/21/04	Renee Rosnes Quartet
11/23/04 – 11/28/04	Lou Donaldson Quartet
11/30/04 – 12/5/04	Bill Frisell Quintet
12/7/04 – 12/12/04	Bill Frisell Quintet
12/14/04 – 12/19/04	Roy Hargrove and Cedar Walton Quartet
12/21/04 – 12/26/04	Cedar Walton Quartet
12/28/04 – 1/02/05	Dr Michael White's Original Liberty Jazz Band
1/4/05 – 1/9/05	Jeff (Tain) Watts
1/11/05 – 1/16/05	Paul Motian's Electric Bebop Band
1/18/05 – 1/23/05	Branford Marsalis Quartet
1/25/05 – 1/30/05	Geri Allen Trio
2/1/05 – 2/6/05	Geri Allen Trio
2/8/05 – 2/13/05	Buster Williams Quartet

SEVENTIETH-ANNIVERSARY CELEBRATION

2/15/05	Roy Hargrove Quintet
2/16/05	Wynton Marsalis Quartet
2/17/05	The Bad Plus
2/18/05	Jim Hall Duo
2/19/05	The Heath Brothers (Jimmy, Percy, and Tootie Heath)
2/20/05	Bill Charlap Trio
2/22/05 – 2/27/05	Jeremy Pelt Quintet
3/1/05 – 3/6/05	Wessell Anderson Quartet
3/8/05 – 3/13/05	Bill McHenry Quartet
3/15/05 – 3/20/05	Roy Haynes Quartet

3/22/05 – 3/27/05	Tom Harrell Quintet
3/29/05 – 4/3/05	Kurt Rosenwinkel Quintet
4/5/05 – 4/10/05	Bill Charlap Trio
4/12/05 – 4/17/05	Bill Charlap Trio
4/19/05 – 4/24/05	Carol Sloane
4/26/05 – 5/1/05	Lou Donaldson Quintet
5/3/05 – 5/8/05	Uri Caine Trio
5/10/05 – 5/15/05	The Vanguard Jazz Orchestra [fortieth anniversary]
5/17/05 – 5/22/05	Bobby Hutcherson Quartet
5/24/05 – 5/29/05	Clary Terry Quintet
5/31/05 – 6/5/05	Paul Motian Trio 2000 + 1
6/7/05 – 6/12/05	Mulgrew Miller Trio
6/14/05 – 6/19/05	Ben Riley's Monk Legacy Septet
6/21/05 – 6/26/05	Don Byron
6/28/05 – 7/3/05	Barry Harris Trio
7/5/05 – 7/10/05	Eric Reed Trio
7/12/05 – 7/17/05	Buster Williams and Something More
7/19/05 – 7/24/05	Jimmy Greene Quintet
7/26/05 – 7/31/05	Fred Hersch Trio
8/2/05 – 8/7/05	Bill McHenry Quartet
8/9/05 – 8/14/05	Al Foster Quartet
8/16/05 – 8/21/05	Slide Hampton Sextet
8/23/05 – 8/28/05	Greg Osby Quartet
8/30/05 – 9/4/05	Brian Blade Fellowship
9/6/05 – 9/11/05	Paul Motian, Joe Lovano, and Bill Frisell
9/13/05 – 9/18/05	Paul Motian, Joe Lovano, and Bill Frisell
9/20/05 – 9/25/05	The Bad Plus
9/27/05 – 10/2/05	Jason Moran and the Bandwagon
10/4/05 – 10/9/05	Bill Charlap Trio
10/11/05 – 10/16/05	Bill Charlap Trio
10/18/05 – 10/23/05	Geoffrey Keezer Trio
10/25/05 – 10/30/05	Tom Harrell Quintet
11/1/05 – 11/6/05	Robert Glasper Trio
11/8/05 – 11/13/05	Bebo Valdés

11/15/05 – 11/20/05	Lou Donaldson Quartet
11/22/05 – 11/27/05	Brad Mehldau Trio
11/29/05 – 12/4/05	Jim Hall Trio
12/6/05 – 12/11/05	Jim Hall Trio
12/13/05 – 12/18/05	Joe Lovano's Expanded Ensemble of 11
12/20/05 – 12/25/05	Cedar Walton Quintet
12/27/05 – 1/1/06	Dr. Michael White and the Original Liberty Jazz Band
1/3/06 – 1/8/06	Jimmy Greene Quartet
1/10/06 – 1/15/06	Kurt Rosenwinkel Group
1/17/06 – 1/22/06	Jeff "Tain" Watts
1/24/06 – 1/29/06	Paul Motian Band
1/31/06 – 2/5/06	Joe Wilder Quartet
2/7/06 – 2/12/06	Barry Harris Trio
2/14/06 – 2/19/06	Bill McHenry Quartet
2/21/06 – 2/26/06	Jeremy Pelt Quartet
2/28/06 – 3/5/06	Fred Hersch
3/7/06 – 3/12/06	Wallace Roney Sextet
3/14/06 – 3/19/06	Roy Haynes Quartet
3/21/06 – 3/27/06	Kenny Barron Trio
3/28/06 – 4/2/06	Tom Harrell Quintet
4/4/06 – 4/9/06	Paul Motian Quartet
4/11/06 – 4/16/06	Billy Hart Quartet
4/18/06 – 4/23/06	Bill Frisell Quintet
4/25/06 – 4/30/06	Bill Frisell Quintet
5/2/06 – 5/7/06	Dave Douglas Quintet
5/9/06 – 5/15/06	Fly (Mark Turner, Larry Grenadier, Jeff Ballard)
5/16/06 – 5/21/06	Renee Rosnes Quartet
5/23/06 – 5/28/06	Robert Glasper Trio
5/30/06 – 6/4/06	Eric Reed Trio
6/6/06 – 6/11/06	Uri Caine Trio
6/13/06 – 6/18/06	Guillermo Klein/Los Gauchos

6/19/06	Sweet Lorraine: A Jazz Celebration for the Village Vanguard** Guests: The Vanguard Jazz Orchestra, with saxophonist Joe Lovano; Roy Hargrove Quintet, with the vibraphonist Bobby Hutcherson; Paul Motian Trio 2000 + 1, with Chris Potter, Larry Grenadier, and Rebecca Martin; Dr. Michael White's Original Liberty Jazz Band; and the Bad Plus
6/20/06 – 6/25/06	Lewis Nash Quartet
6/27/06 – 7/02/06	Paul Motian Band

DISCOGRAPHY

1989

Kenny Burrell Quartet (8/1/89 – 8/6/89)
Guiding Spirit [Fantasy]
Harper Brothers Quintet (9/5/89 – 9/10/89)
Remembrance [Verve]

1990

Christian Escondé/Pierre Michelot Quartet
   (10/30/90 – 11/04/90)
Live at the Village Vanguard [Emarcy]
Geri Allen, Charlie Haden, Paul Motian (12/18/90 – 12/23/90)
Live at the Village Vanguard [DIW]

1991

Benny Green Trio (11/05/91 – 11/10/91)
Testifyin' [Blue Note]
Sun Ra Sextet (11/12/91 – 11/17/91)
At the Village Vanguard [Rounder Records]

1992

**Dr. Michael White's Original Liberty Jazz Band of New
   Orleans** (12/31/91 – 1/05/92)
New Year's at the Village Vanguard [Antilles]

Arthur Taylor's Wailers (8/25/92 – 8/30/92)
Wailin' at the Vanguard [Verve]

Joshua Redman, Pat Metheny, Charlie Haden, Billy Higgins
(9/1/92 – 9/4/92)
Wish [Warner Bros.], only two tracks were recorded at the
Village Vanguard

Geri Allen Trio (10/20/92 – 10/25/92)
Live at the Village Vanguard [DIW]

1993

Arthur Blythe Quartet (6/22/93 – 6/27/93)
Retroflection [Enja]

David Murray Trio, (8/17/93 – 8/22/93)
[Unissued]

Kenny Burrell Quartet (8/24/93 – 8/29/93)
Midnight at the Village Vanguard [Evidence]

Vincent Herring Quintet (11/23/93 – 11/28/93)
Folklore [BMG/Musicmasters]

1994

Junko Onishi Trio (5/3/94 – 5/8/94)
Live at the Village Vanguard, Vol. 1 [Blue Note]

Live at the Village Vanguard, Vol. 2 [Blue Note]

Hamiet Bluiett Quartet (7/19/94 – 7/24/94)
Live at the Village Vanguard: Ballads and Blues [Soul Note]

Wynton Marsalis Septet (3/6/90 – 3/11/90), (7/2/91 – 7/07/91),
(11/30/93 – 12/5/93), (11/29/94 – 12/4/94)
Live at the Village Vanguard [Columbia], seven-disc set

Selections from the Village Vanguard [Columbia], box set

Eastern Rebellion (12/20/94 – 12/25/94)
Just One of Those Nights at the Village Vanguard
[BMG/Musicmakers]

1995

Joshua Redman Quartet (3/21/95 – 3/26/95)
Spirit of the Moment [Warner Bros.], two-disc set

Paul Motian Trio (6/06/95 – 6/11/95)
You Took the Words Right Out of My Heart [JMT]

Slide Hampton and the Jazzmasters (8/1/95 – 8/6/95)
Dedicated to Diz [Telarc]

1996

Joe Lovano Quartet (3/19/96 – 3/24/96), (3/26/96 – 3/31/96)
Live at the Village Vanguard [Blue Note]

Jim Hall Trio with Guests (12/3/96 – 12/08/96)
Panorama: Live at the Village Vanguard [Telarc]

1997

Tommy Flanagan Trio (3/04/97 – 3/16/97)
Sunset and the Mocking Bird: The Birthday Concert [Blue Note]

Brad Mehldau Trio (7/29/97 – 8/03/97)
The Art of the Trio, Vol. 2 [Warner Bros]

McCoy Tyler Trio (9/23/97)
McCoy Tyler Plays John Coltrane [Impulse]

Paul Motian Trio (9/16/97 – 9/21/97)
Sound of Love [Winter & Winter]

1998

Wessell Anderson Quintet (5/26/98 – 5/31/98)
Live at the Village Vanguard [Leaning House Jazz]

1999

Brad Mehldau Trio (1/5/99 – 1/10/99)
Art of the Trio: Back at the Vanguard [Warner Bros.]

Chucho Valdés Quintet (3/30/99 – 4/11/99)
Live at the Village Vanguard [Blue Note]
Chucho Valdés Solo: Live in New York [Blue Note]

2000

Brad Mehldau Trio (9/19/00 – 9/24/00)
Progression: Art of the Trio, Vol. 5 [Warner Bros.]

Mary Stallings with Eric Reed Trio (9/26/00 – 10/01/00)
Live at the Village Vanguard [MaxJazz]

2002

Jason Moran Trio (11/26/02 – 12/1/02)
[Unissued]

2003

Uri Caine Trio (5/20/03 – 5/25/03)
Uri Caine Trio: Live at the Village Vanguard [Winter & Winter]
Fred Hersch Trio (8/19/03 – 8/24/03)
Live at the Village Vanguard [Palmetto Records]

INDEX